S0-ENU-924

TQ 120 B

# TQ 120 B
## BLACKABY

BROADMAN & HOLMAN PUBLISHERS

NASHVILLE, TENNESSEE

**TQ120B**

Copyright © 2005 by Henry Blackaby and Richard Blackaby

All rights reserved

ISBN 13: 978-0-8054-3069-1
ISBN 10: 0-8054-3069-5

Broadman & Holman Publishers
Nashville, Tennessee
www.broadmanholman.com

Unless otherwise noted, all Scripture quotations have been taken from the *Holman Christian Standard Bible*® Copyright © 1999, 2000, 2002, 2003 by Holman Bible Publishers.

Dewey Decimal Classification: 242
DEVOTIONAL LITERATURE

Printed in the United States of America
1 2 3 4 08 07 06 05

# TABLE OF CONTENTS

SERMON FOR TODAY ................................................. 1

MARY'S CHRISTMAS ................................................ 21

SAVED IN SIN CITY .................................................. 29

LIFE-CHANGING EXPERIENCES ................................ 59

DAVID'S STORY ....................................................... 67

THE FAITH WORKOUT .............................................. 97

NEWS YOU CAN USE ............................................. 115

DEEP-DOWN DEVOTION ........................................ 135

WANT TO START AGAIN? ....................................... 143

# INTRODUCTION

Could there be anything more exciting than to wake up each morning, knowing you're going to meet with God? How incredible to think that you can talk directly with the Creator of the universe, telling him your problems and listening to what he has to say about them!

Yet that's exactly what you can do each day, because God invites you to spend time with him! You are free to tell him whatever is on your heart. You can ask him any question and find comfort from any pain. God promises to respond to you with love. This makes meeting with God something you ought to look forward to each day with tremendous anticipation.

This *TQ120* devotional book is meant to assist you as you meet daily with God. It assumes you already have a personal relationship with him through faith in Jesus Christ. If you do not, you can begin a relationship with him by praying and asking God to forgive you of your sin. Then commit yourself to doing whatever he tells you.

This devotional book has Scripture verses that will introduce you to wonderful promises from God that can change your life. As you read the devotions, be sure to have your Bible with you, because although we've done our best to make our words valuable, God's Word to you is vital!

Also, keep a pen with you so you can write your thoughts in the journaling sections—because when the Lord of the universe says something to you, it's important enough to write down! Later, you can look back over the things God has said to you during your times with him and see how he has been leading you, day by day. This will make this book a great source of comfort to you as you see how God has been guiding you and sharing his love with you.

Commit yourself to spending regular time with God each day. It will change your life!

# SERMON FOR TODAY

Never had anyone encountered a man like Jesus! Everywhere he went, he explained the Scriptures, preached the good news, and made sick people well.

Lots of rabbis taught in the synagogues. People had been listening to them for years. But none taught with the authority, grace, and power Jesus did! The other teachers droned on and on about keeping the law, making God seem farther and farther away, cold and inaccessible, but Jesus taught about freedom and forgiveness. Other preachers had come and gone, but Jesus was in a class by himself. He seemed to understand the Scriptures as no one ever had before.

Perhaps most amazing to the crowds was his healing power. With a mere word or touch, Jesus could cure deafness, blindness, paralysis, epilepsy, and leprosy. He could even cast out demons, liberating people who for years had been in bondage to cruel, evil spirits. No wonder the crowds followed him!

On one occasion, they followed him partway up a mountain to hear what he had to say to his disciples. As they gathered around, with their hearts and ears anxious to hear his words of wisdom, Jesus taught them with spellbinding insights into God's Word. Scholars have named this particular message the Sermon on the Mount, found in one bulk section of Matthew (chapters 5–7), as well as sprinkled throughout the Gospel of Luke. For the first seventeen days of our devotional journey through this *TQ120* book, we'll spend some time with the profound wisdom of the greatest teacher in history—Jesus Christ.

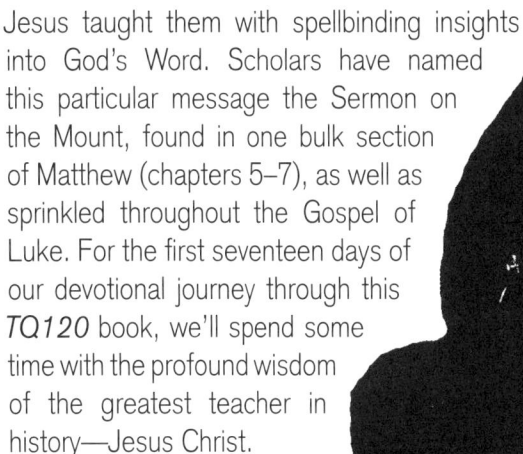

# LISTEN UP

### READ AHEAD: MATTHEW 5:1-2
*Then He began to teach them, saying . . .* Matthew 5:2

Everywhere Jesus went, masses of people followed. The sick would cry out loudly for healing. People would jostle one another to get a closer look at him. They'd press in on him, trying to touch him and be healed.

As news spread about this miracle worker, people from surrounding cities dropped what they were doing and rushed to Galilee to see for themselves. It never took them long to locate Jesus. The noise around him had grown to a deafening pitch.

But one day, as the crowds closed in around the disciples, all became quiet. Then Jesus delivered the greatest sermon in human history—what scholars have named the "Sermon on the Mount." Actually, Jesus was teaching his twelve disciples, but the nearby crowds were also treated to the most profound teaching ever heard.

This same Jesus is your Teacher. He has wisdom to share with you that will astound you, just as it did to those who heard him with their own ears. You don't have to be sitting in a quiet sanctuary or a Sunday school class for him to teach you, though you can learn from him in both of those places. He can teach you something no matter where you are, even in a noisy crowd.

Do you understand who your Teacher is? He is the Christ, the Lord of the universe! Pay close attention when he speaks so you don't miss a word he has for you!

## WHAT WOULD YOU SAY TO PEOPLE WHO TELL YOU THAT GOD DOESN'T COMMUNICATE WITH US?

### READ UP: PSALM 119:97-104 • ISAIAH 30:19-21

# PATH TO PROSPERITY

**READ AHEAD: MATTHEW 5:3–12**

*Blessed are the poor in spirit, because the kingdom of heaven is theirs.* Matthew 5:3

For the next few days, we'll be looking at a special section of the Sermon on the Mount (verses 3–12) called the "beatitudes" (pronounced, be-AT-itudes). These are promises of blessing, short statements that teach us what pleases the heart of God. The first of these is found in verse 3: "Blessed are the poor in spirit."

Financial advisers say that if you want to become rich, you should live like a pauper. Many billionaires are famous for their chintzy lifestyles. They live in modest homes and drive ordinary cars. They consistently live below their means, investing the money they don't spend. It seems that underestimating one's worth is apparently a key to financial prosperity.

This kind of humility is also one of the keys to *spiritual* prosperity. Many falsely assume their spiritual bank account is full simply because they're good people, go to church on Sunday, and try not to hurt anyone. They conclude that God must be pleased with them because of their goodness. But all the good deeds in the world won't cover a person's spiritual debt before God.

Jesus said we inherit the kingdom of heaven only when we recognize our inability to pay our spiritual debt. When we admit our spiritual poverty, realizing that without Christ we are spiritually destitute, only then do we become wealthy. By assuming the attitude of a pauper, we become poor in spirit . . . while building up a limitless bank account in heaven!

## WHERE DOES HUMILITY RANK ON THE PRIORITY LISTS OF MOST OF THE PEOPLE YOU KNOW?

**READ UP: DANIEL 4:18–37 • REVELATION 3:17–19**

# SAD TO SAY

## READ AHEAD: MATTHEW 5:3–12

*Blessed are those who mourn, because they will be comforted.*
Matthew 5:4

If the first step to spiritual growth is humility, as Jesus said in the first of his beatitudes (verse 3), the second step is repentance—grieving over our sin. Jesus referred to it as *mourning*.

Mourning is usually associated with death. When someone dies, we mourn the loss as a way of dealing with our emotional anguish. Grief counselors say that unless we mourn during a time like this, we'll never begin the healing process.

Jesus said essentially the same thing concerning sin. Until we face the gravity of our sin head-on, grieving over its devastating power, we will never find healing from it.

Some people want to skip over this grief stage because sin can be so depressing to deal with. They'd rather hurry along to the part about becoming a new creation. They don't want to see their sin for what it is, so they try to gloss over it. But Jesus said we must see our sin the way God sees it—as being deadly, devastating, and destructive. Only when we grieve over the depravity of our soul's sinful condition will we find comfort and renewal in Christ.

If you've been taking your sin lightly or finding excuses for it, there's something you haven't understood. Sin—*your* sin, *all* our sin—is what cost Jesus his life. When you understand this truth until it breaks your heart, then you're ready for your next step up the mountain.

## WHAT HAPPENS TO US WHEN SIN DOESN'T REALLY BOTHER US ANYMORE?

**READ UP: ISAIAH 29:13–16 • LUKE 22:55–62**

# STRENGTH UNDER CONTROL

**READ AHEAD: MATTHEW 5:3–12**

*Blessed are the gentle, because they will inherit the earth.*
Matthew 5:5

Generations of comic strip fans knew the inside scoop on Superman. Meek and mild Clark Kent was really Superman in a very thin disguise, consisting primarily of a pair of thick-rimmed eyeglasses. Clark was meek, but he certainly wasn't weak. In fact, he went to great lengths to hide the superhuman power behind those spectacles.

In a similar (but much more spiritual) way, the third beatitude teaches us that the "gentle . . . will inherit the earth." Those who surrender their lives to the control of the Holy Spirit will experience God's matchless power working in their lives.

When this happens, you'll have the ability to forgive others, which requires much stronger character than getting revenge. You'll have the moral strength to overcome sin and temptation. Your life will be defined by self-control, not insecurity.

Jesus himself provided the ultimate demonstration of meekness. Though he was the Son of God, he willingly surrendered himself to his enemies in order to save the human race from its own destruction. Though his tormentors mocked him for lacking the power to come down from the cross (Mark 15:30), Jesus showed infinitely more strength by remaining on the cross rather than crying out to his Father to rescue him.

Don't be reluctant to let the Holy Spirit control your life. His strength in you is evidence that you're growing more and more like him.

## WHAT'S SURPRISING TO YOU ABOUT MEEKNESS BEING SEEN AS A STRENGTH?

**READ UP: PSALM 37:8–11 • PHILIPPIANS 2:5-11**

# HUNGRY?

### READ AHEAD: MATTHEW 5:3-12

*Blessed are those who hunger and thirst for righteousness, because they will be filled.* Matthew 5:6

The word *appetite* usually makes us think of food. Actually, though, it comes from the Latin word *petere*, meaning "to seek." An appetite is any strong desire that compels us to go after something.

We can crave all sorts of things: food, love, attention, intimacy, power, money. These appetites can be good or bad . . . sometimes both. And when our appetites are tuned to the wrong things, we will always suffer for it.

Have you grown discouraged by failing God in some way? Are you disappointed with yourself for allowing peer pressure to coerce you into sinning? Maybe you've tried so many times to overcome a sinful habit, you've resigned yourself to living with failure. You think you're powerless to overcome it.

Jesus has a word for you: Don't give up! If you truly desire a life that pleases God, keep seeking after it. You'll find it!

Now that you're a Christian, God's desire is for you to seek or pursue righteousness, to become more and more like Christ. This is why he has given you his Holy Spirit—to cause a deep craving for holiness to grow within you, to tighten your conscience when you sin against him. So you can be sure that when your driving appetite is to please God, he will help you live what you desire, even if you go through many failures in between. If you're genuinely longing for spiritual victory, Jesus says you will be satisfied.

## WHICH COMES FIRST— OBEDIENCE OR THE DESIRE TO OBEY?

### READ UP: 2 CHRONICLES 15:10-15 • ISAIAH 58:13-14

## FREE TO FORGIVE

**READ AHEAD: MATTHEW 5:3–12**

*Blessed are the merciful, because they will be shown mercy.*
Matthew 5:7

At some point in our lives, we all need mercy. We all mess up. We all say foolish things that are better left unsaid. Every one of us has done something we wish we could go back and undo. When that happens, we know we deserve to pay the consequences for our thoughtlessness. The friend we let down shouldn't trust us again. The parent we disobeyed should punish us. The person we've offended should never forgive us.

Do you remember times like these, times when you braced yourself for the worst, yet you were met with loving forgiveness instead? Do you remember how thrilled you were to be given another chance?

Jesus doesn't want you ever to forget what it's like to receive mercy when you deserve condemnation, to be saved when you deserve to be left for dead. So when the shoe is on the other foot, when you're the one who's on the receiving end of the hurtful words or the offensive behavior, stop and think about mercy. Sure, your friend said a nasty thing. Yes, your sister did an irresponsible thing. But remember this: Jesus warned that you'll be treated with the same measure of mercy that you give to others (Matthew 7:1–2).

When you're willing to extend mercy to others, no matter how badly they've treated you, you're another step up the mountain to maturity—another step closer to being like Jesus.

## HOW DO YOU MAKE MERCY MORE THAN A BIBLICAL CONCEPT, BUT A FLESH-AND-BLOOD REALITY?

**READ UP: GENESIS 50:15–21 • JAMES 2:12–13**

# WHAT DO YOU SEE?

### READ AHEAD: MATTHEW 5:3–12
*Blessed are the pure in heart, because they will see God.*
Matthew 5:8

Many people have concluded that God doesn't exist. If he did, they say they should be able to see some evidence. They act on the assumption that God is obligated to make his presence known to them.

The truth is, God is not obligated to reveal himself to anyone. He *chooses* to do so. Over and over, the Bible gives the assurance that those whose hearts are pure will see God, while those who close their hearts to him will not.

When Jesus walked on earth, teaching the crowds and healing the sick, many people believed the Messiah was in their midst. But others who saw the same miracles and heard the same message were equally unconvinced, thinking he was an impostor! It was the same Jesus. The difference was in the way they saw him.

The question, then, is not whether God makes his presence known, but whether you're able to see him. He's there! So if you've been blind to God's activity all around you, it's time to open your eyes! From the beginning of time, he has made it clear that if we seek him first above all else, we will see him as he really is.

Don't let sin obstruct your vision of God and of who he is. Ask him to reveal every sinful thought or attitude within you so you can get rid of it. When your heart is pure and your motives are right, you will see God—and you'll never be the same again.

## WHY CAN'T WE SEE GOD AND HOLD ON TO OUR SINFUL HABITS AT THE SAME TIME?

### READ UP: 2 SAMUEL 22:26–27 • HEBREWS 12:14–17

# PEACE

**READ AHEAD: MATTHEW 5:3–12**

*Blessed are the peacemakers, because they will be called sons of God.* Matthew 5:9

Have you ever noticed a strong family resemblance between a child and a parent, only to be surprised to discover that the child is adopted? Even when families adopt cross-culturally, family members can grow to resemble one another. That's because similarity is not just physical. It's seen in the subtle things—gestures, expressions, pet phrases. Families spend so much time together that without realizing it, they take on a certain collective identity.

God's family is no different. Certain behaviors should characterize each one of us. We should all be kind, gentle, loving, forgiving, patient, and conspicuous for our self-control.

We should also be known for our desire to bring peace. The world should be able to count on Christians to foster unity and togetherness, not division. Being a peacemaker isn't always easy, because we can be shot at from both sides. But our model is Jesus. He gave his life to give us peace with God.

Today's beatitude—the seventh of eight steps toward Christlikeness—is truly one of the Christian's highest callings. If you're growing in your faith, this means your school, your workplace, and your home should be more peaceful because of your presence. If you're more prone to stir up dissension than to bring peace, you're not living up to your family name. Bring peace where there is division, and Jesus said it will be obvious whose child you are.

**WHICH SINS AND BAD ATTITUDES CONTRIBUTE TO OUR FAILURE IN THE PEACEMAKING AREA?**

**READ UP: EPHESIANS 2:11–18 • JAMES 3:13–18**

# FAITHFUL UNDER FIRE

### READ AHEAD: MATTHEW 5:3–12

*Blessed are those who are persecuted for righteousness, because the kingdom of heaven is theirs.* Matthew 5:10

Imagine you were one of the disciples listening to Jesus' Sermon on the Mount. And let's suppose (like all good students) you were taking notes. Maybe they'd read something like this:

*Eight Steps toward Spiritual Maturity*

| QUALIFICATIONS | EXPECTATIONS |
| --- | --- |
| 1. Poor in spirit, humble | kingdom of heaven |
| 2. Mournful over sin | comfort |
| 3. Meek, gentle | the earth |
| 4. Craving righteousness | being filled |
| 5. Merciful | mercy |
| 6. Pure in heart | will see God |
| 7. Peacemakers | known as children of God |
| 8. Persecuted | *blessing (?)* |

Hold it a minute! How, by anyone's imagination, could persecution be a blessing? But wait, Jesus said it again (verse 11): "Blessed are you when they insult you and persecute you and falsely say every kind of evil against you because of Me." He said persecution is cause to rejoice, because the rewards for such suffering will be great in heaven. So when you're ridiculed and rejected for your faith, remember Jesus' words. Persevere to the top of the mountain, and your reward in him will be great.

## IF THIS IS TRUE, THEN WHY NOT JUST GO AROUND MAKING ENEMIES?

### READ UP: JOHN 15:18–21 • HEBREWS 11:24–26

# TASTE TEST

### READ AHEAD: MATTHEW 5:13–15

*You are the salt of the earth. But if the salt should lose its taste, how can it be made salty?* Matthew 5:13

Salt was considered so valuable in Jesus' day that it was sometimes used for money. (That's where we get the phrase, "He's worth his salt.") Among the things salt was prized for:

- *It kept food from rotting.* Meat preserved with salt stayed fresh longer.
- *It brought out the taste in food.* A sprinkle of salt could give bland food better flavor.
- *It possessed healing properties.* Applying salt to a wound helped it heal much faster.

In the same way, Christians help to preserve other people from sin and destruction. It may be that your friend is being tempted to sin, but you urge him to resist. Every time you do that, you're keeping him from the destructive effects of sin.

Christians are also equipped to add flavor to life by bringing joy to those around us. The world should be a better place because we are in it.

Finally, we are one of God's instruments for bringing healing to people. When hurting people come to us, we can share God's love with them. In doing so, we help restore hope and comfort to their wounded souls.

That's why it's crucial that we fulfill God's intention by enriching the lives of others, never losing our edge—our saltiness—in serving Christ. Just as salt was highly valued in Jesus' time, we are called to make a valuable difference in the lives of those around us.

## CAN YOU THINK OF ANOTHER ANALOGY OR TWO TO DESCRIBE A CHRISTIAN'S INFLUENCE?

### READ UP: COLOSSIANS 4:5–6 • 1 PETER 4:7–11

# LIGHTEN UP

**READ AHEAD: MATTHEW 5:13-15**

*You are the light of the world. A city situated on a hill cannot be hidden.* Matthew 5:14

Few things are as important to people as light. When we want to be secure from crime, we turn on lights. When we can't see things clearly, we turn on a light.

Can you imagine a world where everything was darkness and no one had the assurance of seeing where he was going or what others were doing? People who are deprived of light often become sick, depressed, and even suicidal.

Jesus described Christians as light—as light in a dark and hopeless world. There are things that cover people's lives with darkness, such as sickness, loss, guilt, and failure. But those who live in darkness need hope. That's why God has provided them with a Christian influence—with us—to be a light for them, pointing them to Christ. As we allow his light to shine through us, we are able to brighten the outlook for those in spiritual darkness.

No problem is so black that God cannot bring victory, and no sin is so evil that God cannot forgive it. As a Christian, you have the opportunity to be light in a darkened world. Everywhere you go, you can be enlightening people about him. You can help people say, as C. S. Lewis wrote many years ago, "I believe in Christianity as I believe that the sun has risen—not only because I see it, but because by it, I see everything else." Will you be that light today?

## WHAT SPECIFICALLY ABOUT CHRISTIANITY IS LIFE-GIVING AND LIGHT-INDUCING?

**READ UP: JOHN 12:44-46 • PHILIPPIANS 2:14-15**

# THIS WAY, THAT WAY

## READ AHEAD: MATTHEW 5:21-22

*You have heard that it was said . . . but I tell you . . .*
Matthew 5:21-22

Everyone has an opinion about what's right and wrong. Listen to a call-in program on any number of subjects, and you'll hear the whole gamut of opinions. One caller will be adamantly in favor of something, and the next caller will be vigorously opposed to the same thing. But both are convinced they know the truth!

In Jesus' day the law was very important. The Ten Commandments and the other ancient Scriptures provided the definitive word on what was right and what was wrong. As far as the Jewish people were concerned, this was God's final word on any subject.

Then along came Jesus, who took the Scriptures to a completely new level. He didn't dispute what the law teachers taught. He just expanded it, presenting God's Word not only in terms of what it said about outward practice but also what it said about the heart.

• *The law said not to murder?* Jesus said don't even entertain hatred for someone.

• *The law said not to commit adultery?* Jesus said don't even lust in your heart.

• *The law allowed you to get revenge on your enemies?* Jesus said to love them.

If God's Word differs from what you're hearing, you know which one to believe.

**WHAT ARE SOME OF THE BIG SPIRITUAL QUESTIONS YOU HEAR PEOPLE ARGUING ABOUT?**

## READ UP: PSALM 119:33-40 • JOHN 8:30-32

# FIRST THINGS FIRST

### READ AHEAD: MATTHEW 5:23-24

*First go and be reconciled with your brother, and then come and offer your gift.* Matthew 5:24

Nothing was more important to a Jew than worshiping God. The nation of Israel since Old Testament times had offered sacrifices as a way to show reverence for God. There was no better place to be than kneeling before him at the altar.

So how these words of Jesus must have shocked them!

Jesus said if you're in the midst of worship and you realize that someone is angry or offended at you, stop worshiping and go mend the relationship. After you've made things right, only then will God be interested in your gift.

It is so easy to try satisfying God with our good deeds—going to church, attending a Bible study, living a moral life—while refusing to be reconciled with someone who is upset with us. But Jesus' message to us couldn't possibly be any clearer. He's not asking for nominal attempts at reconciliation, where we offer a feeble or partial apology: "I'll admit I was wrong if you will" or "I tried to patch things up, but she was still angry." He's calling us to restore the relationship completely, no matter who was right and who was wrong, no matter how long it takes. Then we can return gladly to worship, with hearts free from guilt or bitterness. Then our offering will mean something.

Before you attend another worship service, is there someone with whom you need to be reconciled?

## WHAT CAUSES MOST OF THE RIFTS BETWEEN YOU AND YOUR FRIENDS, YOUR SIBLINGS, YOUR PARENTS?

### READ UP: PSALM 15:1-5 • COLOSSIANS 3:12-15

# NOBODY'S PERFECT?

### READ AHEAD: MATTHEW 5:43–48

*Be perfect, therefore, as your heavenly Father is perfect.*
Matthew 5:48

When you read this verse, you might think something was lost in the translation. Perhaps Jesus meant to say that we should be as close to perfect as we can be. No, Jesus said it is possible to be perfect.

This doesn't mean you will never make mistakes. Being "perfect"—biblically speaking—means to be complete, lacking in nothing. It means to reach spiritual maturity. It means that the same things which characterized Jesus' life should characterize ours. In other words, to be perfect means to be like Christ.

A tall order? You bet. But God wants you to fill it.

Throughout history, the human race has accepted a lower standard than God's standard. Our sin has caused us to fall short of becoming the people he meant for us to be. The Bible is filled with accounts of those who chose to disobey God instead of cooperating with him, and it always led to their destruction.

We still do it today. We still don't trust God to make us complete, so we choose our own way. We do what we think is best, and we get what we bargained for. Jesus said it doesn't have to be that way. God has a plan to make us spiritually mature. We just have to trust him and follow it. If we will allow him, he will rid us of every selfish and sinful attitude in our hearts. Then he'll remake us into the image of his Son.

**WHO'S SOMEONE THAT FITS THIS DEFINITION OF PERFECTION? WHAT IS HE OR SHE LIKE?**

### READ UP: 1 KINGS 8:54–61 • ROMANS 6:6–11

# MONEY TROUBLES

### READ AHEAD: MATTHEW 6:19–21
*For where your treasure is, there your heart will be also.*
Matthew 6:21

Your heart can be a battleground! And whoever (or whatever) owns it will determine what you do with your life.

One of the great temptations you'll face in life will be in the area of money and possessions. The world will bombard you with advertisements of wonderful things you could buy if only you had enough money. Slick advertisements will promise that your life would be perfect if only you had a particular product. Society will affirm that whoever has the most money will be the happiest and most powerful. The world can make the pursuit of money and possessions very tempting!

But Jesus has some warnings for you if you are preoccupied with gaining wealth: Wealth doesn't last. Money doesn't satisfy. It is only temporary. Possessions can be stolen. Money can be lost or wasted. Even if you do obtain wealth, you will find that it disappoints, because it cannot truly satisfy you.

Jesus taught that true happiness comes not from collecting possessions but from investing our lives in things that are eternal. Spiritual things last forever. No one can take them away. They don't depreciate over time. Investing in God's kingdom is the smartest investment anyone could ever make.

Where have you been investing your time and effort? Have you set your heart on things that will last forever?

## WHAT HAVE YOU NOTICED ABOUT PEOPLE WHO VALUE THEIR STUFF MORE THAN THEIR RELATIONSHIPS?

### READ UP: PROVERBS 23:4–5 • ECCLESIASTES 5:10–20

# QUICK TO CONDEMN

### READ AHEAD: MATTHEW 7:1–5
*Do not judge, so that you won't be judged.* Matthew 7:1

Jesus warned us not to judge one another, because the standard we use to judge others will be the same standard used to judge us.

This doesn't mean we can never say anything when someone else is sinning, or that we can never engage our minds and Christian convictions when declaring things we know to be true from God's Word. Some people like to quote this verse as an excuse to do whatever they want without being corrected, or as an easy way out of defending a biblical position. That way, they can claim the moral high ground while bending to the pressure of being totally tolerant of others.

That's not what Jesus meant when he warned us not to judge. He was addressing the wrongful attitude of immediately condemning someone without hearing all the evidence, of showing no mercy to someone who's done wrong. This kind of attitude takes delight in seeing others get what's coming to them, rather than grieving over the pain and loss their sins have generated for them.

Remember, God is perfectly fair. It's *his* job to judge people's actions and the motives behind them, not ours. So we've been duly warned. If we act as a judge over others, we'll be measured by the same harsh standards we use to condemn. So be as generous as you can with your attitude toward others, and God will respond with grace toward you.

## WHY IS THIS ONE OF TODAY'S FAVORITE VERSES—FOR CHRISTIANS AND NON-CHRISTIANS ALIKE?

### READ UP: ROMANS 14:10–12 • JAMES 4:11–12

# HEARING VS. LISTENING

**READ AHEAD: MATTHEW 7:24–27**

*Everyone who hears these words of Mine and acts on them will be like a sensible man who built his house on the rock.* Matthew 7:24

Hearing and listening are two completely different things. *Hearing* is a physical process in which sound waves go into your ears, vibrate for a while, then head for your brain. *Listening* is a mental process. It's what your brain does with the message it gets.

A deaf person may not hear, but she can be an excellent listener. On the contrary, a hearing person may have sound waves entering his head, but that doesn't make him a good listener.

Jesus explained the huge difference between hearing and listening by using the analogy of two men who were both building houses. The first man understood that a house built on a solid foundation could withstand the storms when they came. The second man—too foolish to plan ahead and too lazy to consider what a storm could do—built his house on sand. So when the storms came, the same rain and the same wind that pelted the two houses had a different effect on each. The first man's house was unshaken, while the second man's house fell with a mighty crash.

Don't be like the foolish builder. Don't think your job is done once you've heard what Jesus has to say. When you hear a great message or read a profound truth in your Bible, it's nothing more than a sound wave tickling your eardrums unless you apply what you hear. The evidence that you've listened to God's Word is a changed life. Are you listening?

## HOW DO YOU "LISTEN" TO THE WORD OF GOD?

**READ UP: PSALM 50:16–23 • JOHN 15:9–10**

# HOW WOULD YOU DESCRIBE JESUS' TEACHING?

# MARY'S CHRISTMAS

Twenty centuries ago, when the Jewish people were expecting the Messiah, the highest honor a family could hope for was that this Promised One would be born into their family line. Young women from wealthy families harbored the hope that they might be the one chosen to give birth to the Savior. It made sense that such a hero would be raised in a noble family with all the advantages money and position could offer.

Mary, however, didn't have either of these. She was just a young teenager when her parents arranged her marriage to a man much older than she was. No doubt she expected her life to follow a fairly predictable path—rearing her children and living quietly as a carpenter's wife in the backwater town of Nazareth.

But while Mary may have seemed like an ordinary young woman to most of the people who knew her, God saw her in a totally different light. He saw a heart that was devoted to him. He saw a gentle girl who trusted him.

He saw the perfect woman to nurture the Son of God.

This average teenager could never have imagined what God would do through her life. For many centuries afterward, her name would symbolize godly love and devotion. She would become a biblical model for humility and total surrender to God.

We can learn much from examining her life, because her example shows how God can work through ordinary people to do amazing things. Not just at Christmas, but every day of the year.

# ONE ORDINARY GIRL

**READ AHEAD: LUKE 1:26–29**

*In the sixth month, the angel Gabriel was sent by God to a town in Galilee called Nazareth.* Luke 1:26

God dispatched an angel with an incredible message for Mary, a small-town girl planning a small-town wedding and a small-town life. Of all the women of her day—or of any age before or after—God had chosen her to bear the Savior!

Mary was under no delusions. She was neither the prettiest nor the wealthiest woman in the world. She was smart but uneducated. And she was so young! She still had much to learn about life. Predictably, she was completely taken by surprise when the angel Gabriel relayed this awesome assignment.

Why did God choose Mary? Because he saw her humility and her quiet faithfulness to do what he asked of her. This was exactly the kind of person he could trust to raise his Son. Outward things—looks, money, power—none of these mattered. What mattered was a heart yielded to do the will of God.

You may see some similarities between your life and Mary's. You may be going about your life expecting all the ordinary things: finishing your education, finding a job, getting married, having children. But in the midst of your ordinary life, God may surprise you with something extraordinary. You may not consider yourself to be anyone special, but God does. He sees your heart. He knows how faithful you've been to him. He may decide he can trust you with something unusual. Seek to be faithful, and watch expectantly to see what he does in your life!

## WHAT MAKES AN ORDINARY PERSON SUCH FERTILE GROUND FOR GOD TO WORK IN?

**READ UP: 2 SAMUEL 7:18–24 • 1 CORINTHIANS 1:26–31**

# BIGGER THAN WE ARE

### READ AHEAD: LUKE 1:30–33

*The angel told her, "Do not be afraid, Mary, for you have found favor with God."* Luke 1:30

When God shows you what he wants to do with your life, it may scare you to death! The angel he sent to Mary terrified her. Before Gabriel could tell her of the plans God had for her, he had to calm her down first. Even then, his message overwhelmed her! It was too hard to take in!

If God were to reveal to you everything he has in store for your future, you too might be overwhelmed. That's why he usually tells you only what he wants you to do right now. So whatever God has asked you to do next, don't be afraid. Just obey.

And even if what he is asking of you seems too hard, don't limit him. Don't think of your situation in human terms. When God does things, they are God-sized. They are impossible for you to do apart from his help. If there is nothing unusual about your life right now, perhaps it's because you've been leaving God out of it.

Nothing is as exciting as walking closely with God. Those who think the Christian life is boring are not living it the way God intended! Walking with him will stretch you in ways that nothing else will.

So trust him and don't fear. As you obey him—step by step, day by day, week by week, year by year—you will look back on your life and be amazed at where he's taken you and what he's done.

### WHAT HAS GOD BEEN ASKING OF YOU LATELY THAT SEEMS TOO HARD FOR YOU TO DO?

### READ UP: JUDGES 6:11–16 • JEREMIAH 32:24–27

# IS IT POSSIBLE?

**READ AHEAD: LUKE 1:34–38**

*For nothing will be impossible with God.* Luke 1:37

Has God ever spoken to you about something he wanted you to do and you thought, "But that's impossible"?

The angel Gabriel was telling Mary about a plan that not only *sounded* impossible; it *was* impossible! Surely she could not be expecting a baby. She was still a virgin! Surely God would not choose a mere human being to give birth to his holy Son! Surely God wouldn't let peasants raise the Son of God!

Yet that's exactly what God was planning. For though these things were indeed humanly impossible, they were entirely possible for the Lord. He created life itself. Why should anything be beyond his ability to do it?

Read Gabriel's words closely, though. He didn't tell Mary, "Nothing is impossible for you if you try hard enough!" Nor did he say, "You can do anything if you just believe in it enough." He said, "When God wants to do something, nothing is too difficult for him. Nothing can stop him."

God can do anything he wants in your life. He can get you a job. He can help you overcome an addiction. He can protect you from harm. He can even change your heart!

Has he told you something he wants to do in your life? Do you believe him? The moment you say, "But that's impossible!" you have revealed what you really believe about God.

Remember, with God all things are possible!

## HOW CAN YOUR LIFE BECOME LIVING PROOF THAT GOD CAN DO THE IMPOSSIBLE?

**READ UP: MARK 9:17–24 • ACTS 4:13–14**

# HIS WAY

### READ AHEAD: LUKE 2:1–7

*She gave birth to her firstborn Son, and she wrapped Him snugly in cloth and laid Him in a feeding trough.* Luke 2:7

Things don't always work out the way you thought they would, do they? You've probably experienced occasions when you were expecting something good to occur, but when the time came, it ended up being sort of disappointing or embarrassing.

Perhaps, though, those things happened exactly as God wanted.

If you had been Mary or Joseph—expecting the Messiah, the Savior of mankind—what kind of expectations would you have had? Not a cattle shed with a feeding trough for a cradle! Even a modest hotel room would have been better than a cold barn! Instead of nurses by her side, Mary ended up with some rough, dirty shepherds, who probably smelled as bad as the barn did.

No, things didn't pan out exactly as Mary and Joseph would have wished. They may have even felt like failures. Maybe they thought it was their fault for not providing a better birthplace for a King. But Jesus' birth happened precisely according to God's plan. He *wanted* his Son to be born in a lowly and humble setting—completely the opposite of what generations of hopeful Jews had expected.

When less-than-expected circumstances happen in your life, and you wonder why God allowed this to happen, trust him anyway. Don't be disappointed. Don't be embarrassed. God never does things the way we would have done them. His way is always better!

## WHAT MAKES US HESITANT TO LET GOD DO THINGS HIS WAY?

**READ UP: ISAIAH 55:8–11 • JEREMIAH 42:5–6**

# WHAT DOES MARY'S EXAMPLE SAY TO YOU?

# SAVED IN SIN CITY

Sometimes we think following Christ was somehow simpler in Bible times than it is today. Have you ever assumed that the people who populated the early church had an easier time being godly than we do today in our evil society?

Well, if Hollywood ever made a movie about the church in Corinth, it would receive the strictest of ratings! There was gross immorality in that church, not to mention pride, selfishness, and divisiveness. You name a sin—they were dealing with it.

Why did this church struggle so much? For one thing, it was located in a very ungodly city. Corinth was famous as a seacoast destination for sailors from all over the world, who came ashore to find diversion and excitement. The city was wealthy, offering every form of entertainment and temptation imaginable. Even the Greek temples that existed there were immoral. They actually employed prostitutes to ply their trade in the temple buildings as a form of worship. Things were as bad as you could possibly imagine. Yet the Christians of Corinth were trying to live faithfully for Christ.

The Bible never tells only the good things while glossing over the bad. The Bible tells things the way they were . . . and are. Paul's two letters to the believers in Corinth were painfully honest about the changes necessary if the Christians living there were going to honor Christ while surrounded by such vulgarity.

Can you identify with the Corinthian Christians? Does your environment pressure you to abandon your Christian values and join the crowd? As you read Paul's straightforward advice to the Corinthian church, remember that these words were written to Christians like you, Christians who were trying to honor God in an environment that was as ungodly and immoral as any place you will find today.

# TWO SIDES, SAME CROSS

**READ AHEAD: 1 CORINTHIANS 1:18–25**

*To those who are perishing, the message of the cross is foolishness, but to us who are being saved it is God's power.*
1 Corinthians 1:18

Don't be surprised when not everyone is as excited about the gospel as you are! As you enjoy the thrill of walking with Jesus, you may be surprised when others choose not to experience God in the same exciting way you do.

Paul understood that those who approach Christianity with skepticism will never find any power in it. Such people consider the gospel foolishness. On the other hand, those who truly believe the good news discover firsthand the power of God.

Why is it some people never experience God's activity in their lives? Because their lack of faith prevents them from seeing him at work. Their rejection of the truth ultimately costs them their lives. However, those who approach God with faith see him at work, and they experience his mighty power on a regular basis.

The Bible says some people simply refuse to accept the truth of the cross. To nonbelievers the Christian message is nonsense, so it holds no power for them. They can't understand how *anyone* could accept it. They may even ridicule *you* for believing it!

But never stop sharing the good news simply because some people reject it. There will be those who do accept the truth of Christ, and you will see them experience God at work in their lives in the same powerful way he has worked in yours.

## WHY WOULDN'T GOD JUST KNOCK EVERYBODY DOWN WITH HIS TRUTH?

**READ UP: ROMANS 1:16–17 • TITUS 3:3–7**

# WHAT'S INSIDE?

**READ AHEAD: 1 CORINTHIANS 2:10–16**

*We have not received the spirit of the world, but the Spirit who is from God.* 1 Corinthians 2:12

Part of the fun in giving gifts is already knowing what's inside! At Christmastime, don't you enjoy thinking of just the right thing to give those who are close to you, picturing the look on each person's face as he or she opens your token of love?

God enjoys giving gifts, too. In fact, each Christian has a storehouse brimming with good things God wants to give us.

Along with eternal life, the first gift we receive when we become Christians is God's Holy Spirit. In fact, if it were not for the presence of God's Spirit within us, we would never know about or experience the many other blessings God wants to give us.

God does not intend for us to struggle in our own power or settle for less than his best for us. He has treasures that will meet our every need if we will just ask. He wants to give us courage to calm our fears, peace to erase our anger, joy in place of sadness, forgiveness to remove our bitterness, and much more. The Holy Spirit leads us into all of these.

Are you now enjoying the good gifts your Father has for you? Or are you living in your own strength, unaware that God has a much better plan? Listen to the Holy Spirit within you. He will make you aware of all the blessings God has made available for you. Find out what's inside the package.

## WHAT WOULD BE DIFFERENT ABOUT OUR CHRISTIAN WALK IF THE HOLY SPIRIT WASN'T INSIDE US?

**READ UP: PSALM 25:4–5 • JOHN 16:13–15**

# TRIAL BY FIRE

**READ AHEAD: 1 CORINTHIANS 3:10–15**

*Each one's work will become obvious, for the day will disclose it, because it will be revealed by fire.* 1 Corinthians 3:13

Life holds only a certain number of days for each of us. As each new day arrives, we begin to spend it hour by hour, minute by minute. The clock ticks away whether we want it to or not. We have no choice about spending the time. The only choice we have is in *how* we will spend it. Will we invest it *accidentally* or *intentionally*?

Those who choose to live without intentionality squander their days on meaningless activity. They give little thought to their spiritual lives. They care only for things that have earthly value, things that yield temporary satisfaction. Their goal is basically not to have a goal.

Living intentionally, however, means putting your energy into things that help you grow as a Christian—like reading this devotional today, for instance. It means studying your Bible, praying, being involved in your church, and helping others know God. Some people don't see the point in exerting all this effort . . . but one day they will.

The Bible tells us that on the day of judgment, God will test our lives with fire, stripping away everything that has no eternal significance. Earthly honors will evaporate. Sports accomplishments will disappear. Material wealth will be gone. All that will remain will be our love for God, our love for others, and the time we spent in prayer, sharing the gospel, and using our gifts to bring him glory. These things will last. These are the things worth pursuing.

## WHAT DOES THE REALITY OF A COMING JUDGMENT MAKE YOU FEEL LIKE AND THINK ABOUT?

**READ UP: MALACHI 3:2–4 • REVELATION 20:11–12**

# HIGH-PRICED HOUSES

**READ AHEAD: 1 CORINTHIANS 3:16–17**

*Don't you know that you are God's sanctuary and that the Spirit of God lives in you?* 1 Corinthians 3:16

If you've ever been to a royal palace, you noticed how perfectly everything is kept. The lawns are neatly manicured. The furniture is in place. The floors gleam. The whole place is immaculate. An entire team of housekeepers and gardeners works full-time to make sure everything is groomed and in perfect working order for the monarch. Every room is decorated with exquisite art and costly furnishings.

That's because kings and queens don't live in run-down shacks. They inhabit palaces.

God, the King of the universe, has chosen you as his dwelling place. He wants to make your body a place of residence for his Holy Spirit. This makes your body holy. But do you treat it that way? Is everything in order for the King? Or have you abused the temple of God by allowing impure thoughts to flood your mind? Have you insulted the King by dulling your senses with drugs and alcohol? Have you taken your body to places where it will be tempted by the enticements of this world?

As a Christian, you take God's Spirit with you everywhere you go. Since it is God's dwelling place, your body is a holy and special place. Don't think less of your body than God does. Treat your body as the holy temple that it is, and use it to bring glory to God in all that you do.

## WHAT KINDS OF THINGS HAVE YOU ALLOWED TO JUNK UP YOUR "TEMPLE"?

**READ UP: ROMANS 6:12–14 • TITUS 2:11–14**

# LOOKING THE WRONG WAY

**READ AHEAD: 1 CORINTHIANS 4:1-5**

*Don't judge anything prematurely, before the Lord comes.*
1 Corinthians 4:5

When people hurt you or offend you, do you review their behavior over and over in your mind, analyzing what would make them do such a thing?

It's natural to wonder what's behind someone else's actions, especially when his conduct causes pain in our lives. It's easy to ascribe motives and assume the worst. We often want to see our offender receive a fitting punishment for treating us badly.

Although it's tempting to judge other people this way, it's not biblical. Only God knows what's truly in people's hearts. He alone understands what motivates people to do what they do. Furthermore, he tells us in clear terms to leave the analyzing to him.

So we can waste a lot of time figuring out the imperfections in those around us, or we can just do as Paul says and wait until "the Lord comes." It's much wiser to focus on our own character, working on the things we need to change, than to waste time worrying about others getting what they deserve.

A day is coming when God will judge every person for what he or she has done. In the meantime, then, don't invest a lot of time or energy worrying about the sins of others. Concentrate instead on keeping your own life pure before God, and then you will enjoy God's praise . . . no matter what other people try to do to you.

## WHAT REALLY MOTIVATES US TO JUDGE PEOPLE PREMATURELY?

**READ UP: PSALM 9:7-10 • ACTS 5:34-39**

# POWER BEYOND WORDS

**READ AHEAD: 1 CORINTHIANS 4:18–20**

*For the kingdom of God is not in talk but in power.*
1 Corinthians 4:20

As Christians, we often talk and sing about the powerful God we serve. Yet when we come up against challenges to our faith, we sometimes start to backpedal furiously: "Sure, God can do anything he wants, but I'm no spiritual giant. I'm just an average run-of-the-mill person."

We need to reread the Bible! It's filled with accounts of ordinary men and women God empowered to do great things! Joshua was an ex-slave who defeated every army he faced. Esther showed incredible bravery, putting her life on the line for her people. Elijah challenged the queen and her army of hostile pagan priests by calling down fire from heaven.

Were these all unusually rugged people, gifted with supernatural bravery and endurance? Not at all. They were ordinary people whose strength came from God.

So if this same God who defeated armies and destroyed entire cities now lives within you, there's no reason why your life shouldn't reflect his awesome power. You don't need to feel intimidated by those who oppose your Christianity. Don't let anyone or anything frighten you out of obeying God. When God calls you to follow him, he empowers you to accomplish his desires.

Walk closely with almighty God, and let his power shine through your life. Trust in the infinite strength of the one who lives within you. Don't just talk about the power of God. Experience it!

## WHAT'S SOMETHING YOU TALK ABOUT IN SPIRITUAL TERMS, BUT YOU DON'T REALLY LIVE?

**READ UP: 2 CHRONICLES 20:5–12 • EZRA 8:21–23**

# GOOD CHOICE

### READ AHEAD: 1 CORINTHIANS 6:12–13

*"Everything is permissible for me," but I will not be brought under the control of anything.* 1 Corinthians 6:12

Not everyone in the world is free. Some are in bondage to dictatorships, restricted from anything that goes against their government's wishes. Others live out their days in prison, paying their penalty for breaking the law. There is another kind of bondage, however, that doesn't involve being enslaved by others. This bondage involves the restrictions people place on themselves by their own choices.

Paul said he had once been a prisoner of sin. Sin had placed such a grip on his life that he didn't even realize how enslaved he was. It wasn't until after he became a Christian that he experienced true freedom for the first time.

There were Christians in Paul's day, though, who abused their new-found freedom and unwittingly became slaves again. They thought that if God had already made a place for them in heaven, why not indulge in any sin they wanted to, without worrying about their eternal destiny? Do you see the stupidity in this? Why would someone who had been freed from a terrible taskmaster turn around and walk right back into captivity?

Having experienced both slavery and freedom, Paul was determined that sin would never again entrap him in its lies. Even though he was free to make his own choices, he would only choose those things that honored God. We do well to follow his example. Don't ever take lightly the freedom that Christ bought for you on the cross.

## WHAT ARE SOME THINGS THAT ARE "PERMISSIBLE" FOR YOU BUT ALWAYS LEAD TO TROUBLE?

### READ UP: ROMANS 6:1–4 • GALATIANS 5:13–15

# DOING WITHOUT

### READ AHEAD: 1 CORINTHIANS 8:7–13

*If food causes my brother to fall, I will never again eat meat, so that I won't cause my brother to fall.* 1 Corinthians 8:13

It's easy to become frustrated with Christians who are weaker in their faith than you are. But they don't need your criticism. They need your encouragement.

In Paul's time, animals were sacrificed to idols in pagan temples. After the animal had been offered to the gods, the temple priests would then sell the meat in the local market. Some Christians didn't have a problem buying this meat for food. Others, though, refused to have anything to do with it, knowing it had been used in idol worship. You can see, then, where the controversy and name-calling came in.

Personally, Paul wasn't troubled by where the meat came from. He knew that the idols were merely pieces of stone or wood, and he considered the meat nothing more than a good bargain. Yet he knew that eating it could scandalize Christians who disagreed with him.

He could have said, "Well, that's their problem," and dismissed their viewpoint. But he considered unity more important than who was right or wrong, so he chose not to eat the meat. Though his own conscience freed him to partake of it, he chose to refrain so he didn't cause a weaker Christian to be offended.

Is there something you're doing that younger Christians find objectionable? Are you causing another believer to stumble in his faith? Are you mature enough to give up some of your freedom in order to live in harmony with your fellow believers?

**KNOWING THAT SOME WILL BE OFFENDED BY ANYTHING, HOW DO YOU DRAW THE LINES IN THIS AREA?**

### READ UP: LUKE 17:1–2 • ROMANS 13:8–10

# WHO NEEDS TO KNOW?

### READ AHEAD: 1 CORINTHIANS 9:19–23

*I have become all things to all people, so that I may by all means save some.* 1 Corinthians 9:22

What are you willing to do to help someone know Christ? Are you willing to establish a friendship with someone who is totally different from you, perhaps someone of another ethnic background or a lower social class? What if the two of you have nothing in common and you don't identify with the person at all?

Maybe you assume God wants you to befriend only those people with whom you feel comfortable. You figure if he wants to reach someone you don't understand and who shares different interests, surely he will work through someone else!

Isn't it a good thing Jesus didn't make that assumption about us? What did God's Son, seated on his throne in heaven, have in common with us? Yet when he saw our need, the holy and perfect Son of God became human like us, so he could communicate the good news of salvation with weak and sinful humanity.

Paul was determined to find a way to identify with whomever he could, just so long as he could tell them about God's salvation. Paul was as comfortable telling kings about Jesus as he was beggars.

Are you willing to go out of your way, strike up a conversation, or begin a friendship with someone—even though they may be very different from you—so you can tell them about Christ? Who knows, you might even discover there aren't as many differences between you as you thought!

## WHO'S SOMEONE YOU'VE SHIED AWAY FROM WHEN IT COMES TO SHARING CHRIST?

### READ UP: ACTS 10:28–34 • 2 TIMOTHY 2:24–26

# GOD'S GYM

**READ AHEAD: 1 CORINTHIANS 9:24-27**

*Run in such a way that you may win.* 1 Corinthians 9:24

No Olympic medalist will ever tell you the prize came easily. Successful athletes spend years undergoing extensive training, preparing for the day when they will match their abilities against other competitors to see who's the fastest and strongest. But to the athlete, the prize is well worth the many hours spent in training. Good things seldom come without a cost.

This truth also applies in the spiritual world. When you read about the spiritual giants in Christian history, or when you admire the strong faith of your pastor, don't assume you have no chance to enjoy the same walk with God as they do. You possess just as much opportunity to walk closely and powerfully with God as they have.

The question is this: Are you willing to pay the same price they were in order to be filled with God's powerful presence? Are you willing to make the sacrifices of wise choices? Are you willing to put in the time it takes to follow God completely?

Spiritual strength doesn't come without hard work and exercise. You cannot be spiritually lazy and vibrant at the same time. It's not possible to neglect reading your Bible and ignore the place of prayer in your life and still become a strong Christian. There is a price to pay for having an intimate walk with God. But if you're willing to do whatever is necessary in order to run the race of the Christian life well, the prize will be more than worth your effort.

> **WHAT ARE SOME OF THE HARDEST PARTS OF YOUR DAILY WALK WITH CHRIST?**

**READ UP: PROVERBS 22:3–6 • HEBREWS 5:11–14**

# ESCAPE PLAN

### READ AHEAD: 1 CORINTHIANS 10:6–13

*God is faithful and He will not allow you to be tempted beyond what you are able.* 1 Corinthians 10:13

There's no way around it: you are going to face temptation. You can go to church regularly, read your Bible faithfully, and pray diligently, but you will be tempted to sin just the same.

Still, temptation catches some Christians by surprise. They find themselves in a compromising situation, and they don't know what to do. Then before they know it, they've given in to sin. They may try to excuse their actions, pleading that they were caught off guard. They may claim they were overtaken by the one sin they're powerless to resist.

Nonsense! The Bible says we will never face a temptation that we can't overcome. No matter what it is, God will provide a way for us to escape without sinning.

The problem is, we don't *want* to resist some temptations. We ignore the warning signals and walk right past the escapes God has provided for us. Then we find ourselves in the clutches of a powerful temptation and cry out at the last minute, "God, save me!" But it's too late. How much wiser to listen to God at the outset when he first cautions us of the danger!

Don't ever take temptation lightly. Listen to the warnings of others who love you. Take the escape route that God provides. Don't rush headlong into sin, assuming you are too weak to resist anyway. You can live a victorious life if you will listen to the one who can give you victory.

## REMEMBER A TEMPTING SITUATION WHERE GOD PROVIDED YOU AN OUT— AND YOU TOOK IT?

### READ UP: GENESIS 39:1–12 • EPHESIANS 6:10–17

# ALL FOR ONE

### READ AHEAD: 1 CORINTHIANS 10:25–31

*Whether you eat or drink, or whatever you do, do everything for God's glory.* 1 Corinthians 10:31

You don't have to be a missionary or a martyr to glorify God. You can bring glory to God simply by living a transformed life—a life that demonstrates the unmistakable presence of the holy God who lives within you. It's not that God *needs* the glory your holy life brings him, but he does delight in receiving it. When people see how you live and marvel at the goodness of your God, you are bringing glory to him.

God is accustomed to receiving glory for his wonderful creation. The vast expanse of the universe, the majestic mountains, the peaceful lakes, the gigantic canyons . . . all of the wonders of his creation compel us to praise him for his marvelous works.

But we, too, are God's creations capable of bringing him glory. When others watch us love and forgive people as Jesus did, serving rather than seeking to be served, maintaining peace in the midst of turmoil, and giving the glory to God for our righteous deeds and character, they will be moved to praise God for his transforming power. When people see how God turns sinners like us into people who look like Christ, God will receive the glory.

God has given you so much. And if you're looking for a way to say thanks, there's no need to do anything spectacular. You can give something back to him simply by living a life that brings him honor. This is what glorifies God!

> WHY DO WE OVEREMPHASIZE BIG SPIRITUAL FEATS, WHILE PLAYING DOWN ORDINARY OBEDIENCE?

### READ UP: MICAH 6:6–8 • MARK 12:28–34

# WANT TO BE LIKE YOU

### READ AHEAD: 1 CORINTHIANS 10:32–11:1

*Be imitators of me, as I also am of Christ.*
1 Corinthians 11:1

Are you aware of the effect others have on you? We're all influenced by other people, whether we realize it or not—sometimes for good and sometimes for bad. Someone who claims to be his own person, boasting that no one else has any impact on him, is living in denial.

The question is not, "*Will* someone influence me?" but "*Who* is going to influence me?"

So who are your role models? Paul understood that the ultimate role model is Christ. So as Paul labored to be like Christ, he urged others to follow his example. Paul wasn't boasting. He just understood that the only things in his life worth emulating were the things that were like Jesus. Paul's desire was not that they be like him but like Christ.

We often choose our role models unwisely. We idolize sports heroes or other celebrities, knowing very little about their character. Then we are crushed to discover that our heroes are not all we thought they were.

Take stock of who exerts the most influence in your life right now. Is it someone whose example you'd be better off not following? Are you willing to consider ending an unhealthy relationship that regularly drags you away from Christ, making it harder for you to follow him? It's important to be smart about the role models you choose. Seek out those who by their example will show you how to be more like Jesus.

## HOW MOTIVATED ARE YOU TO BE A GOOD ROLE MODEL FOR THOSE WHO NEED ONE?

### READ UP: JOHN 6:66–69 • 1 JOHN 2:3–6

# CHURCH FUNCTIONS

**READ AHEAD: 1 CORINTHIANS 12:12–20**

*God has placed the parts, each one of them, in the body just as He wanted.* 1 Corinthians 12:18

There are times when we wish we could spend time with Jesus, not just spiritually but physically. We want to see him, touch him, hear his voice. We wish we were like those privileged few apostles who spent time with him, day in and day out.

God has a provision for this desire. It's called the church.

When Jesus ascended physically to heaven, God established the church to be the body of Christ on earth, a flesh-and-blood expression of his love. It's not a haphazard group of people, thrown together with no purpose other than getting together on Sunday mornings. It's much more than that! God lovingly puts each church body together with a purpose. He brings to each church specific people who will help the body more accurately reflect the character of Jesus.

Everything Jesus did while he walked on the earth, he chooses to do now through his body, the church. Just as Jesus had compassion for sinners, the church today should have compassion for sinners. Just as Jesus brought salvation to people, so people should be led to Christ through the church. Just as Jesus fed and ministered to the poor, so the poor ought to have their needs met by the church.

If you're not presently part of a church body, seek the church God wants you to join. Then ask his direction for how to get involved. God has a reason for placing you there.

## WHEN DOES YOUR CHURCH MOST SEEM TO RESEMBLE WHAT GOD INTENDED FOR IT?

**READ UP: EPHESIANS 4:11–16 • 1 THESSALONIANS 1:7–10**

# GROW UP

### READ AHEAD: 1 CORINTHIANS 13:1–13

*When I was a child, I spoke . . . thought . . . reasoned like a child. When I became a man, I put away childish things.*
1 Corinthians 13:11

There are a number of advantages to being a little kid. For one thing, not a lot is required of you. No one gives you too much responsibility because, of course, you can't handle it yet. You're allowed to be more self-centered than adults are. In fact, adults are expected to cater to your wants and needs! Your job is just to play and make messes. All in all, it's a pretty good life.

But, of course, no one remains a child forever. As you grow older, more is expected of you. Life brings responsibility, work, and sacrifice. Yet growing up also brings many joys and pleasures! With maturity come new experiences, and life takes on new meaning.

When we become Christians, we are spiritual babies. Regardless of our age at the time of our salvation, we are children in God's kingdom. Unlike our physical bodies, however, our spiritual natures don't mature simply through the passing of time. It's not automatic. A person can be a Christian for thirty years yet still be a spiritual baby.

Some people are satisfied with that. They don't mind being spiritually immature their entire lives. They remain self-centered, interested only in their own happiness and pleasure. But others, like Paul—and like you—are not content to remain spiritual children. You're ready to grow up, to put the extra effort in, to take steps every day that ensure your spiritual maturity. That's what God considers to be the normal Christian life.

## IN WHAT PERIODS OF YOUR LIFE HAVE YOU NOTICED THE MOST SPIRITUAL GROWTH?

### READ UP: PSALM 92:12–15 • 2 PETER 3:17–18

# BAD COMPANY

### READ AHEAD: 1 CORINTHIANS 15:33-34

*Do not be deceived: "Bad company corrupts good morals."*
1 Corinthians 15:33

How strong do you think you are? Are you able to stand up against temptation? Do you think you can resist the opinions and attitudes of those who don't respect the love you have for God?

If you think you can, the Bible has a warning for you. Paul claimed that you will be influenced by the people with whom you spend the most time. If you associate with wise people, you will become wise. If you hang around with fools, they will influence you in the wrong direction. Pretty straightforward, isn't it?

Does this mean, though, that you should never associate with those who hold different beliefs than you do? Of course not. It does mean, however, that you must maintain a real awareness of this truth: both of you are going to have an influence on the other.

Sometimes we argue that we're in a friendship in order to have a Christian influence on a person whose values differ from ours. Maybe we are. It's crucial, however, never to forget that influence goes both ways. At times we can be under someone else's influence far more than we are influencing that person.

Hold up each of your relationships to God and ask for his guidance, remaining always prepared to remove yourself from bad company (as he leads you) if your own character is in danger. At the same time, be looking for people to spend time with who will encourage you to become more like Christ.

## HOW HAVE YOU NOTICED INFLUENCE WORKING FOR OR AGAINST YOU IN YOUR RELATIONSHIPS?

### READ UP: PROVERBS 13:20-21 • PROVERBS 22:24-25

# WE WIN!

### READ AHEAD: 1 CORINTHIANS 15:51–57

*Thanks be to God, who gives us the victory through our Lord Jesus Christ!* 1 Corinthians 15:57

There are plenty of forces at work to defeat you in your Christian life. There are people who wouldn't think twice about causing you to stumble and fail your Lord. There are temptations that could easily destroy your life if given the opportunity. The Bible warns of the "spiritual forces of evil in the heavens" (Ephesians 6:12). It's enough to discourage even the strongest Christian!

But it shouldn't. Do you know why?

Christians should never fear what Satan or the world can throw at us, because Jesus Christ is our Lord, and through him we have the victory. Paul never said trials wouldn't come. Rather, he assured us that in spite of any obstacles, we can be victorious—thanks to Jesus Christ.

Paul experienced this victory himself. When critics taunted him, God affirmed him. When his enemies arrested him, God ministered to him in prison and used him to share the gospel with his warden. Even Paul's execution did not defeat his lifelong passion of telling others about Christ, for to this day millions of believers find inspiration in the letters he wrote to the early church.

If you're looking for a trouble-free life, Paul made no promises. But if you seek victory over God's enemies, it's yours for the asking. You need only to trust God and do what he tells you. When you obey God no matter the cost, you already have your victory.

### WHAT DO YOU DO WHEN VICTORY SEEMS LIKE ANYTHING BUT A FOREGONE CONCLUSION?

### READ UP: 1 CHRONICLES 29:10–13 • ISAIAH 25:8–9

# NOTHING WASTED

**READ AHEAD: 1 CORINTHIANS 15:58**

*Be steadfast, immovable, always excelling in the Lord's work, knowing that your labor in the Lord is not in vain.*
1 Corinthians 15:58

Whenever you sin, Satan is pleased. When you are lazy and waste your time, Satan is content. But when you commit yourself to doing the work of the Lord, mark this: Satan is vehemently opposed to you.

Yes, life can often be the hardest when you're trying to do the right thing. When you make a commitment to obey what God is asking you to do, you might come up against a lot of opposition. Perhaps it will come from your friends. Maybe your parents will even try to discourage you from obeying what God is telling you to do. Whatever it is, you'll be tempted to ask, "Why me? I'm just trying to do what God told me to do!"

Paul would say two things to you about this:

• *First, he would urge you to stand firm.* Paul, of all people, knew that serving God isn't always easy. Satan always tries to sabotage your efforts. Those around you may not understand what you're doing. But Paul would tell you not to hold back. Obey your Lord with everything you've got, because there are eternal consequences at stake.

• *Second, remember that your efforts are never in vain.* Don't get frustrated and give up. When you're obeying God and being faithful to your commitment, victory is a given.

If you're facing some difficult times because of your desire to obey God, rest assured. Your efforts are not wasted. God sees your heart, and he will give you the victory.

## WHAT HAPPENS TO BELIEVERS WHO DON'T REALIZE THAT CHRISTIAN LIVING IS A BATTLE?

**READ UP: DEUTERONOMY 32:45–47 • GALATIANS 6:7–9**

# OPPOSITES ATTACK

### READ AHEAD: 1 CORINTHIANS 16:5-9

*. . . because a wide door for effective ministry has opened for me—yet many oppose me.* 1 Corinthians 16:9

Don't expect everyone to be pleased and encourage you as you try to live a victorious Christian life. Sometimes the number of people who are opposing you stands in direct proportion to how much you're doing for God!

When you serve God, you simply have to get used to being *encouraged* and *oppressed* at the same time. Just because you're doing God's will, this doesn't mean you won't have problems. In fact, the very opposite is usually true.

The apostle Paul rejoiced that a new and exciting opportunity had opened up for him to serve the Lord. At the same time, though, there were many opposing him. It seemed, in fact, that there was always something bad cropping up in Paul's life to go along with the good. He chose to focus on the positive, however, instead of the negative. If he had let himself become sidetracked by those who criticized him, he would have missed some of the exciting things God wanted him to do.

Don't ever let your critics rob you of the joy of serving God. There will always be some who stand by and evaluate your life, assuming they know your motives, feeling it their duty to point out your failures. If you let their opinions consume you, you'll lose sight of the good things God is doing in your life.

So always weigh the opinions of others against God's Word. Fix your mind on pleasing him, because his is the opinion that matters most.

## HOW DO YOU KNOW A "WIDE DOOR" OF MINISTRY WHEN YOU SEE ONE?

**READ UP: PSALM 109:1-4 • ACTS 18:5-11**

# WHAT'S THAT I SMELL?

### READ AHEAD: 2 CORINTHIANS 2:14–17

*Thanks be to God, who always puts us on display in Christ, and spreads through us in every place the scent of knowing him.*
2 Corinthians 2:14

Back in the days of the Roman Empire, Roman generals would often hold a victory parade after winning a great battle. In a celebration known as a *triumph*, enemy prisoners would be marched through the streets as evidence of the Roman conquest. During the parade, sweet-smelling incense would be released into the air, signaling to everyone in the area that their general had won a great victory.

Interestingly, the apostle Paul compared Christians, not to the Roman conquerors, but to the captives. He explained that we have been captured by Christ, and now we are his prisoners of war to display to the world his victory over sin. Paul said that through *our* lives—Christ's captives—comes the victory fragrance that alerts others to the presence of our Conqueror. We are the fragrance of life to those who come to know Jesus through our witness. On the other hand (according to verses 15–16), we are the smell of death to those who reject him.

When people meet you, do they have the unmistakable sense that you belong to God? It should be obvious to them that through you they can come to know Christ. The choice is theirs, of course, whether to accept God's love or to reject it, but there should be no doubt by your example that it is available to them.

Ask God to use your life so that everywhere you go, you will fill that place with the knowledge of Christ.

## HOW DOES A BELIEVER LOOK, SOUND, AND SEEM DIFFERENT FROM OTHERS?

### READ UP: PHILIPPIANS 1:27–28 • COLOSSIANS 1:27–29

# SOURCE OF STRENGTH

**READ AHEAD: 2 CORINTHIANS 3:4–6**

*. . . not that we are competent in ourselves to consider anything as coming from ourselves, but our competence is from God.*
2 Corinthians 3:5

Do you sometimes lack the confidence to carry out what God is asking you to do? Do you look at yourself and conclude, "I'm not a gifted person or a Bible scholar. I don't have what it takes to do anything significant for God"?

If you think this way, you're missing the point . . . because the ability to make a difference in God's kingdom never comes from us. It always comes from God.

Take Paul's life as an example. You might wonder how one man could have accomplished all that he did. How did he start new churches in so many places when he was up against such fierce opposition? How did he perform all those miracles? How did he find the strength to keep going in spite of beatings, shipwrecks, imprisonment, and constant danger?

The answer, of course, is that his ability came from God. It wasn't that Paul was a supernatural being. His strength was not in himself but in his relationship with the Lord.

Likewise, God will never ask you to do something difficult and then leave you to do it on your own. The reason you can have total confidence in him is because no matter what Christ tells you to do, he will always provide you with the ability to accomplish it. Is God leading you into a new area of ministry? Then accept his assignment with boldness, for he will enable you to do whatever he asks.

# WHY DOES CONFIDENCE MATTER? CAN YOU SERVE GOD WITHOUT IT?

**READ UP: PSALM 118:5–9 • 1 JOHN 3:21–24**

# GROWING INSIDE

**READ AHEAD: 2 CORINTHIANS 4:16–18**

*Even though our outer person is being destroyed, our inner person is being renewed day by day.* 2 Corinthians 4:16

Teenagers are often teased about how much time they spend in front of the mirror. Actually, people of all ages spend thousands of hours over their lifetimes keeping their bodies presentable: the showers, the haircuts, the teeth brushings. Add it all together, and the time we spend on grooming tasks is pretty substantial.

Yet although we give our bodies the best of care, they are still only temporary and will one day pass away. This doesn't mean you should stop combing your hair, but it's important to keep the right perspective.

Paul was never one to mince his words, like when he wrote: "Our outer person is being destroyed," or "is wasting away." Our souls, however, are eternal and will never grow old.

When we feed our souls on God's Word, when we take time to pray, when we love the people around us, our efforts are never wasted. Rather than withering away, our souls become fresher and more vibrant each day, even as our physical bodies are inching one day closer to death. Every day for as long as we live, our inner selves are able to experience more and more of life as we grow in our relationship to Christ.

Think about how much time you spend caring for your body. Then compare this to the amount of time you spend nurturing your soul. Never forget, your soul will be around long after your body is not. So be sure to take good care of it.

**WHAT MAKES STUDENTS AND TEENAGERS PARTICULARLY BLIND AT TIMES TO THIS LONG-TERM TRUTH?**

**READ UP: PSALM 90:10–12 • ISAIAH 40:30–31**

# NO EXCUSES

### READ AHEAD: 2 CORINTHIANS 5:6–10
*We must all appear before the judgment seat of Christ.*
2 Corinthians 5:10

Have you ever been caught in the act, doing something you shouldn't? Do you remember the shame?

Can you also recall times when you did things you knew were wrong but you *didn't* get caught? Did you still feel guilty about it?

The apostle Paul warned that regardless of whether or not our sins are revealed in this life, no one escapes the scrutiny of the Lord Jesus. Nothing is done behind God's back or without his notice. He sees how we spend every minute, every second of every day.

How should this affect the way we live? It caused the apostle Paul to live with a reverent fear of God. He determined to live a life so blameless that he would not have to dread facing Christ on judgment day. "Whether we are at home or away," he wrote—whether at school or at church, with our friends or our family, on our good days or our bad days—"we make it our aim to be pleasing to Him" (verse 9).

He was also quick to confess any sin in his life so that God would deal with it immediately, not at the judgment. We, too, ought to live with the awareness that one day God will ask us to account for the things we've done, both good and bad.

Is there anything in your life right now that you need to settle with God? If you don't do it now, you'll have to do it later.

## WHY IS THERE OFTEN A GAP BETWEEN WHAT WE KNOW AND WHAT WE DO?

### READ UP: ECCLESIASTES 12:13–14 • LUKE 12:2–3

# RESTART

**READ AHEAD: 2 CORINTHIANS 5:16–17**

*If anyone is in Christ, there is a new creation.*
2 Corinthians 5:17

One of the many exciting things about the Christian life is that it gives us a completely new start. No matter how many sins haunt our past or how deep the scars from old wounds, regardless of how many times we've failed or how stained our reputation is, Christ makes each of us an entirely new person.

Life really does start all over again for the Christian!

When God saved you, he didn't simply add a little spurt of spirituality to your life. Nor did he lay down a set of rules to help you try to curb your sinful habits. He created something absolutely new! He gave you a new heart—a heart that desires to love and serve him. Now that your inner self is renewed, you're empowered to say no to temptation and yes to God.

Many Christians underestimate the radical change that happened when they became God's children. They assume they're still the same sinful, weak, unfaithful people who couldn't live the Christian life even if they wanted to. That is not true! At the moment of your conversion, you became a totally new person embarking on a brand-new life. Past failures can no longer hold you back. Earlier sins have no power over you anymore.

Never forget that in Christ you are "a new creation; old things have passed away, and look, new things have come."

## WHY WAS CHRISTIANITY AN IMPOSSIBLE LIFESTYLE BEFORE WE BECAME BORN AGAIN?

**READ UP: JOHN 3:3–6 • ROMANS 8:5–11**

# WHILE WE'RE HERE

## READ AHEAD: 2 CORINTHIANS 5:18–21

*We are ambassadors for Christ . . . we plead on Christ's behalf, "Be reconciled to God."* 2 Corinthians 5:20

Every time you go out the door, you represent Christ to those you meet. You may assume that you're just going to school, to work, or to be with friends, but you're also on official business to represent your King. Scripture indicates that every Christian is God's ambassador to a searching world.

An ambassador represents his country while living in a foreign place. He tells others what his nation thinks about certain issues. If people want to know the customs of a particular land, they watch the life of the ambassador.

It's incredible that God would appoint us to represent his kingdom. Yet that's exactly what he's chosen to do! If others wonder what God is like, they need only ask us. If they want to know how to contact the King of kings, we should be able to tell them. When those around us watch how we live, they should get a good idea of what God's kingdom is like. If someone we know is hurting, we should be God's messenger of healing. If those around us are rebelling against God, we should be willing to help them reconcile with him.

Just as Jesus showed people what God was like when he walked on the earth, you are now God's earthly representative to a world that doesn't know what God is like. People are watching your life. Take your job seriously and represent him well.

## WHAT ARE SOME OTHER RAMIFICATIONS OF BEING HERE ON TEMPORARY ASSIGNMENT?

**READ UP: EXODUS 19:4–6 • EPHESIANS 6:19–20**

# LIKE NIGHT AND DAY

**READ AHEAD: 2 CORINTHIANS 6:14–18**

*Do not be mismatched with unbelievers. For what partnership is there between righteousness and lawlessness?* 2 Corinthians 6:14

A Christian and non-Christian can never be as close as two Christians can be. That's because Christians live in the light. The Holy Spirit lives within them, causing them to long for what God values and to despise the things God hates. They have willingly surrendered the authority over their own lives to Christ.

Non-Christians, however, live by a different standard. They have neither a love for Christ nor any desire to follow his ways. The Bible describes such people not only as living in darkness but also as enemies of God. Therefore, it is impossible for believers and unbelievers to be compatible.

That's why we Christians must be extremely careful how entwined we become with those who don't share our belief in God. This doesn't mean we shouldn't love nonbelievers or that we should avoid them completely. Yet we shouldn't become so closely tied to nonbelievers that their decisions hinder our walk with God.

Christians must not be fooled into thinking a close relationship with a non-Christian won't affect their love for God. If you marry an unbeliever, for example, your wife or husband's attitudes and practices can dramatically affect your Christianity. It's like adding cold water to hot water. Soon, it all becomes lukewarm and eventually grows cold.

So heed Paul's warning. Don't link your life with anyone who will distract you from loving God.

## WHAT IMPACT DOES PAUL'S ADVICE HAVE ON YOUR FRIENDSHIPS AND DATING RELATIONSHIPS?

**READ UP: EPHESIANS 5:6–12 • JUDE 20–23**

# PRIDE BUSTERS

### READ AHEAD: 2 CORINTHIANS 12:6–10

*Because of Christ, I am pleased in weaknesses . . . for when I am weak, then I am strong.* 2 Corinthians 12:10

The Scriptures are peppered with paradoxes—statements that appear contradictory at first glance:

- If you want to be first, you must be last.
- If you want to live, you must die.
- If you want to receive honor, humble yourself.

These statements don't even seem to make sense—like when Paul said, "For when I am weak, then I am strong."

Paul knew the difference between strength that came from faith in God, and strength that came from relying on his own abilities. He had tried both. Before he met Christ, he oozed self-confidence. As he went about persecuting Christians, he had no doubt in his mind that his life was pleasing to God. Then God humbled him. And after spending three days blind and totally dependent on others to guide him, he was ready to listen and do things God's way.

You, too, may assume you're self-sufficient. You may think you can handle anything life throws at you. But you can be sure that God will one day—if he hasn't already—allow something into your life to reveal the holes in this kind of prideful attitude. For only when you realize how absolutely weak you are without Christ will you ever find yourself on the way to becoming strong.

## WHY DO WE TEND TO ADMIRE PEOPLE WHO COME OFF AS BEING SO SECURE AND SELF-ASSURED?

### READ UP: 1 CORINTHIANS 2:1–5 • 2 CORINTHIANS 13:2–4

# WHAT GOOD HAS SIN EVER DONE FOR YOU?

# LIFE-CHANGING EXPERIENCES

Peter lived on a steady diet of his own words. He was an impulsive, outspoken extrovert, eager to speak his mind and quick to take action. He *meant* well. It's just that his demonstrative personality often got him into trouble!

Peter must have been an exasperating character at times. Yet Jesus never gave up on him. In one of the most memorable of these moments, not long before Peter's well-known denial of Christ, Jesus warned him that Satan would soon be tempting him. Yet Jesus added, "I have prayed for you that your faith may not fail. And you, when you have turned back, strengthen your brothers." Yes, Jesus knew that Peter was going to cave under the pressure, yet he still wanted Peter to know that he loved him, had confidence in him, and would never turn his back on him.

The longer Peter knew Jesus, the more Christ's character became obvious in Peter's life. He developed from a brash, opinionated man into an articulate, confident leader, as seen in his bold sermon on the day of Pentecost (see Acts 2:14–40). Jesus was able to redirect Peter's boldness into a mighty weapon for good. If Christ could work this miracle in Peter's life, there's hope for the rest of us!

As you read Peter's words, take note of the wisdom and maturity that's evident in his writing. Peter is an inspiring example of what Christ can do with a person whose heart is devoted to him.

# BRAIN POWER

## READ AHEAD: 1 PETER 1:10-13

*Get your minds ready for action, being self-disciplined.*
1 Peter 1:13

One big difference between Christianity and cults is that Christianity encourages you to think for yourself, while cults often depend on brainwashing people into following without thinking. Christianity doesn't ask you to stop thinking in order to believe.

Quite to the contrary, the greater thinker you are, the better you will be able to grasp the enormous truths God wants you to understand as a believer. He wants you to love him with all your heart, soul, strength, *and mind* (Mark 12:30). This means he wants you to use your head!

If we allow others to do our thinking for us, we'll always be at the mercy of their opinions and their values. If we waste our days in front of a television set, we'll soak up the world's thinking like a sponge and will never know God the way we should. If our minds are lazy, we'll miss out on so many of the things God wants to teach us! Every Christian ought to be a thinking person.

So make a new commitment today to begin filling your mind with truth so you can't be so easily deceived by Satan's lies. Exercise your brain by reading a good book, renting a thought-provoking movie, spending time with people who know how to think, attending conferences, and asking lots of questions. Look for opportunities to stretch your mind. It takes an active mind to fully appreciate God's greatness!

## HOW DO YOU KNOW SATAN THRIVES ON DECEPTION?

**READ UP: 2 CORINTHIANS 4:1-6 • EPHESIANS 4:22-24**

# EVERYDAY SAINTS

**READ AHEAD: 1 PETER 1:14–16**

*It is written, "Be holy, because I am holy."*
1 Peter 1:16

Being exactly like God could come in handy! If you were all-knowing, for example, you'd never have to study. If you were omnipresent, you could go to school without ever leaving your cozy bed. If you were all-powerful, no one could bully you or take advantage of you.

Yet when God calls you to be like him, he's not talking about these kinds of things. He's talking about being "holy, because I am holy."

Only Christians can do this. Non-Christians can be good, nice, decent, and thoughtful, but they can't be holy. When you accepted Christ as your Savior, God entered your cleansed heart and began living out his life in you. Because God is holy, pure, and good by nature, always operating in truth and love, with no evil at all in him—and because his Spirit lives in you—you now have access to his holiness. You are fully capable of living a holy life.

This means you'll respect God's presence in your life by the choices you make, the movies you see, the books you read, and the company you keep. The way you treat others should be an extension of the way God treats you—with love, patience, and forgiveness. The way you conduct yourself should be worthy of the Spirit of God who lives within you. Being holy doesn't mean striving to follow a list of moral rules. Being holy means living in a way that honors your holy God.

## WHY WOULD GOD PLACE SUCH A HIGH STANDARD ON US?

**READ UP: ISAIAH 4:2–4 • ROMANS 12:1–2**

# EVERYBODY'S JOB

### READ AHEAD: 1 PETER 2:4-10

*You are a chosen race, a royal priesthood, a holy nation, a people for His possession.* 1 Peter 2:9

In Old Testament times, priests did two things:

• *First, they brought God to the people.* That is, they proclaimed God's Word to others and helped people know what God was like.

• *Second, the priests brought the people to God.* They helped those who were searching for God know how to find him and experience his forgiveness.

God has chosen you to be part of his royal priesthood. God wants everyone to know him as you do, so he's called you to act as an intermediary to help others find him.

Many people don't know Jesus personally. They've never spent time with him. They've never read their Bible. They don't know what God is like. But you have a relationship with him, so you can show them who God is. You can help them learn that God loves them and offers them new life through Christ.

You don't need a seminary degree to help others find God. Simply introduce them to your Savior. Even if you don't know your Bible thoroughly, you know enough to help them get started reading theirs. You can tell them what Christ has done for you. You can lead those who are hurting to the one who can heal their pain.

Take God to people, and take people to God. This is what the priests did. And this is what God asks you to do.

## HOW CAN YOUR HOLY, OBEDIENT LIFESTYLE ALONE DRAW OTHER PEOPLE TO CHRIST?

### READ UP: ACTS 9:26-35 • HEBREWS 7:23-25

# WHY WORRY?

**READ AHEAD: 1 PETER 5:1–7**

*. . . casting all your care upon Him, because He cares about you.*
1 Peter 5:7

Anxiety develops when you worry about things beyond your control. Sometimes other people make decisions that affect your life. Awaiting the results of a job interview, for example, can be agonizing because your future is in someone else's hands. Fear of the unknown can cause you anxiety. Days can seem like weeks when you're anticipating a doctor's diagnosis.

But as long as you're clinging to your worries, you're not trusting God to take care of you. He wants you to give your anxiety to him. For even though things may be out of your control, nothing is beyond God's control.

The imagery Peter presented—that of "casting" or *throwing* your cares on God—is not a halfhearted undertaking. It's deliberate and dramatic. It requires a conscious, intentional act of surrender.

Picture yourself beside a lake, holding a fishing rod in your hand. Now imagine that the one, specific worry that's been eating at you lately is attached to that hook. Draw your arm back, then cast your line forward as far as you can. It whirs and flies across the water, and your problem lands way out in the lake.

Now, drop the rod on the beach and walk away.

That's the way God wants you to treat your anxiety. Don't pray to God about your problems and then take them with you at the end of your prayer time. Leave them with God. He can handle them.

## WHAT ARE SOME OF THE BIGGEST PROBLEMS ANXIETY CAN CAUSE YOU?

**READ UP: PROVERBS 12:25–28 • PHILIPPIANS 4:6–7**

# LOOK WHO'S COMING!

**READ AHEAD: 2 PETER 3:8-13**

*The Day of the Lord will come like a thief.* 2 Peter 3:10

There's been endless speculation about Jesus' second coming. Hundreds of books predict when it will be and what it will be like. Speakers travel across the globe sharing their insights into this intriguing event. Many immerse themselves in the topic.

Truly, it is a fascinating subject. In fact, Christ's return has mesmerized people since his resurrection. Even in Peter's day, people were spending a great deal of time speculating on it. But Peter had three simple things to say about the matter:

• *First, God's timing is not like ours.* A thousand years is like a day to God. Using that calculation, Jesus walked the earth only two days ago, and he'll be back sooner than you think.

• *Second, Christ's return will be sudden and unexpected*, like a prowler sneaking into a house under cover of darkness. Thieves don't tell you what time to expect them! Therefore, there's no point in trying to determine exactly when Christ will come.

• *Third, Christ will come in dramatic judgment*, and the world will be no more. Every secret and every sin will be laid bare.

How does all this relate to us? Rather than wasting our time on endless speculations about Judgment Day, we need to understand two things: it is coming, and it will be like nothing we could ever imagine! Let's just live each moment in such a way that no matter when Christ returns, we'll be ready.

## HOW DOES A PERSON REALLY STAY READY FOR CHRIST'S RETURN?

**READ UP: MATTHEW 24:36–44 • LUKE 12:35–40**

# HOW DO YOU LIKE THIS EXPERIENCE SO FAR?

# DAVID'S STORY

David is one of the best-known characters in all the Bible. Even people who don't know the Scriptures all that well can probably tell you about his encounter with Goliath—one of the many Bible stories that's found its way into common knowledge vocabulary.

David's well-known heart of worship and his many deeds of bravery and character provide a strong role model for Christians. Other lessons, however, can be learned by examining his mistakes and striving to avoid them. Either way, David is a fascinating character study, because everyone can relate to his life in some way.

The youngest of Jesse's eight sons, David grew up in a home that was probably considered quite ordinary in his day. He started out tending sheep but proved to be a talented musician and a brave warrior as well. God showed favor toward David, choosing him over all the obvious candidates to be king of Israel. But the crown did not come without a cost. David endured intense adversity on his way to the throne.

Like most of us, David had loyal friends. He also had his share of enemies, people who were sorely jealous of him for a variety of reasons. David could show remarkable wisdom at one point and incredible foolishness at another. He experienced tremendous joy in his life, yet he also suffered grievous heartache. He caused some of his own problems through poor choices, yet—as is common in life—he endured other hardships as a result of his wise, courageous choices.

David's name means "friend of God." Let's spend some time getting to know this fascinating person whom God considered worthy to be his friend.

# WHAT'S ON THE INSIDE?

**READ AHEAD: 1 SAMUEL 16:1–13**

*Man does not see what the Lord sees, for man sees what is visible, but the Lord sees the heart.* 1 Samuel 16:7

David had a few things going against him as candidate for king. First, he was a shepherd, which was not a respected profession. Today we think of them as kind and gentle, but back then shepherds were considered thieves whose word could not be trusted.

Furthermore, as the eighth son in his family, David was a long way removed from the coveted position of eldest son. David was considered so insignificant in his own home that when the prophet Samuel came to choose a king from among Jesse's boys, David was left out in the field watching the sheep! He was the Cinderella of the Old Testament.

Fortunately, however, God doesn't do things the way we do. We're dazzled by outward appearances. We simply assume that the strongest, smartest, most attractive person is the one who naturally deserves the most honor. But God doesn't think that way. He's far more concerned with the condition of our hearts than with the persona we present.

Saul, the first king of Israel, had all the good-looking attributes—the tall physique, the popularity, the influential family. Yet he turned out to have a shallow character. He was a selfish man, plagued by anger and jealousy.

David, however, would prove to be a far better king than Saul. What's even better, David would be known as a man after God's own heart. What an incredible honor for a lowly shepherd boy! But then, that's just the way God does things.

## WHAT HAPPENS TO THOSE WHO GET HUNG UP ON THEIR OUTWARD PACKAGE AND PERSONALITY?

**READ UP: PSALM 147:10–11 • LUKE 16:14–15**

# ONLY THE BEST

**READ AHEAD: 1 SAMUEL 16:14–23**

*I have seen a son of Jesse . . . a valiant man, a warrior, eloquent, handsome, and the Lord is with him.* 1 Samuel 16:18

In many ways we live in an age of mediocrity. We do only what we have to do in order to get by. We try to get the most we can by doing the least we can.

The Bible, though, warns us gravely against this kind of attitude.

When King Saul was looking for someone who could play an instrument, not just anyone would do. He was looking for someone with skill, someone who had practiced and perfected his ability. David was chosen because he could do things well.

As a young person, you have incredible opportunities before you. You have the option of becoming skilled in many areas of life. You can work hard to develop your athletic or musical ability. You can study and make significant contributions to the world of medicine, law, or engineering. You can acquire a diversity of knowledge and skills so that many doors will be open to you in the future.

Some young people accept this challenge to become the best they can be and make a difference in the world. Others, though, look at the cost involved and decide it's not worth it.

Don't be one of those who seeks the path of least resistance. Work hard. Do your best. Take advantage of the numerous opportunities God will give you to be the best you can be. Honor God by your effort, and he will bless you for it.

## WHAT'S USUALLY AT THE END OF THE SHORTCUT OR THE EASY PATH?

**READ UP: PROVERBS 22:29 • ROMANS 16:3–7**

# REMEMBER THE TIME WHEN...

**READ AHEAD: 1 SAMUEL 17:25-37**

*The Lord who rescued me from the paw of the lion and the paw of the bear will rescue me from the hand of this Philistine.*
1 Samuel 17:37

Most things in life are learned by experience. How do you know what pain is, for example? You've experienced it. How do you know what cold feels like? You've felt it. If a friend lets you down again and again, you learn by experience not to trust her anymore. If you're taken in by a con artist, you learn to be more wary of his next scheme.

This principle also applies to our relationship with God. We trust God with a problem today because he was there for us yesterday . . . and the day before that, and the day before that. We pray with confidence now because God has heard our prayers in the past.

If anyone had a track record with God, it was David. So even though it was indeed terrifying to fight a giant—something he had never faced before—he *had* faced a bear and a lion. And God had saved him from death on both occasions. So David had good reason for thinking that God could save him now.

Unless you're a brand-new Christian, you and God have a pretty long history together. Think back over the times when you trusted God to help you. How did he respond? When you faced new and challenging situations, and you called out to God to give you courage, what did he do? As long as you're living in obedience to God, there's never a reason to doubt he'll be there for you. His record speaks for itself.

## WHAT CAN YOU START DOING ON A REGULAR BASIS TO KEEP YOUR GOD-MEMORIES UP-TO-DATE?

**READ UP: PSALM 77:11-15 • ISAIAH 63:7-9**

# THE FIGHT OF YOUR LIFE

### READ AHEAD: 1 SAMUEL 17:41–47

*You come against me with a dagger, spear, and sword, but I come against you in the name of the Lord.* 1 Samuel 17:45

Imagine you were a member of the Israelite army the day young David arrived to challenge Goliath, the Philistine giant. You would've considered David a fool for taking on this menacing monster by using no armor and only a slingshot for a weapon. No doubt the fight would be a short one!

But David wasn't as naïve as everyone thought. Nor was he blind. He could see Goliath towering over all the other soldiers. Even from a distance, he noticed his enemy's enormous weapons—his sword, his spear, and his javelin. He saw how huge the giant's shield was.

Yet David could see other things that the rest of the crowd missed. He could see God's strength, which was far superior to any giant or his weapons.

(Even David, though, apparently underestimated how quickly God would give him victory. He took five stones with him to hurl at Goliath. God needed only one.)

For you, a giant is anything you're facing that seems beyond your power to handle. It may be a tuition payment, an upper-end math class, a term paper, an illness, or a broken relationship you need to mend. What giant are you facing right now? Does it seem enormous? Unbeatable? Don't underestimate how powerful your God is! If you'll trust him as David did, you'll see that God is more powerful than any giant you'll ever face.

## THINK OF ALL THE THINGS THAT MAKE THIS DAVID-AND-GOLIATH FIGHT SUCH A GREAT STORY.

### READ UP: PSALM 18:16–19 • ROMANS 5:6–10

# THAT'S NOT FAIR!

### READ AHEAD: 1 SAMUEL 18:6–16

*Saul was afraid of David, because the Lord was with David but had left from Saul.* 1 Samuel 18:12

Saul had himself to thank for losing God's blessing. He had brought about his own downfall when he became jealous of David, took his eyes off God, and grew envious of the way God blessed David. He couldn't tolerate David being more successful than he was.

David, on the other hand, just continued to keep busy doing what God had asked him to do. And because Saul could see the obvious difference in David's life because of God's blessings, this made Saul even more jealous and self-centered.

Jealousy can start out as a small thing. First, you notice that your friend seems to have something you don't have (like success, talent, or money). That makes you pay closer attention, looking for differences in the way God blesses your friend compared to you. You have an increasing sense of entitlement. *Don't I deserve to have what my friend has?*

And before you know it, you're headed down the same path Saul took, growing angry, bitter, and suspicious of your friend. You look for ways to even the score.

In the end, though, the one who gets hurt the most is you.

Learn from Saul's mistake. He had plenty of reasons to be thankful, but his jealousy blinded him to his own blessings. Don't take your eyes off God to compare your blessings with anyone else's. Choose the path David took—the path of thankfulness—and you'll enjoy God's blessings throughout your life.

## WHAT CAUSES YOU THE MOST JEALOUSY?

### READ UP: MICAH 2:1–3 • 2 TIMOTHY 3:1–5

# WHY ME?

### READ AHEAD: 1 SAMUEL 20:1–9

*What have I done? What did I do wrong? How have I sinned against your father so that he wants to take my life?*
1 Samuel 20:1

David's life was tragic in many ways. He was literally minding his own business when he was plucked from the shepherd's field and made a special assistant to the king. And even though he served King Saul well and could rightfully expect to enjoy the king's favor, he received only his wrath. Rather than appreciating David as a friend, Saul tried to murder him as an enemy.

Why did King Saul hate him so much? It didn't make sense! But David grew to recognize the fact that jealousy and hatred never make sense. Bitterness isn't rational. When people are miserable with their own lives, they become angry and jealous of others' happiness. As the saying goes, "Hurt people hurt people." Poor David was a victim of his own success. The more successful he became, the more Saul hated him.

Don't be surprised if this happens to you, as well. When God honors your obedience, your life will stand in sharp contrast to those whom God is not blessing. They may grow envious of you. They may resent your holy life because it reveals their disobedience for what it is. They may seek to bring you down to their level.

Don't be discouraged. Anytime someone walks with God, he will come across those who resent him. Yet it's always better to walk with God than to settle for lukewarm Christianity . . . no matter what the cost.

## WHY DO OPPOSITION AND RESENTMENT SURPRISE US SO MUCH?

### READ UP: PSALM 10:1–2 • ISAIAH 40:27–29

# BEING THE REAL THING

### READ AHEAD: 1 SAMUEL 22:1–2

*Every man who was desperate, in debt, or discontented rallied around him, and he became their leader.* 1 Samuel 22:2

Attractiveness goes much deeper than our physical features. We've all known some beautiful people who had personalities like rattlesnakes. They were either abrasive, obnoxious, self-centered, shallow, or all of the above. They attracted us initially with their good looks, but we were soon repelled by their personalities.

David was a handsome man, but that wasn't what attracted people to him. The main reason he had a large circle of close and loyal friends was because of his personality.

He was like a magnet for hurting people because he understood their situation. He had been mistreated and misunderstood so many times himself that he was able to sympathize with others. He was always kind and thoughtful, which made people want to be around him. Hundreds of men followed his leadership willingly because they knew he cared about them. No doubt David could have had a face like a can of worms, and he still would have attracted the same people.

Do you have a personality like David's? Do people know that if they're hurting, you will listen and sympathize with them? Or do you unknowingly give off the message that you have time only for those who can help you? If you've been more of a taker than a giver lately, ask God to soften your heart and make you aware of ways to be a friend to someone today. More than likely, you'll receive a blessing in the process!

## WHAT LONG-LASTING TRAITS AND QUALITIES DO YOU VALUE THE MOST IN OTHERS?

### READ UP: PROVERBS 24:1–2 • 1 PETER 2:11–12

# THANKS A LOT!

### READ AHEAD: 1 SAMUEL 23:1–14

*Will the citizens of Keilah hand me over to him? Will Saul come down as your servant has heard?* 1 Samuel 23:11

Have you ever done something nice for someone and then watched him turn against you? It happened to David. As he was fleeing for his life, with King Saul's army in hot pursuit, he became aware of a city under attack by the Philistines. And so he and his little band of warriors—as if they didn't have enough to worry about already—stopped to help the town of Keilah repel its enemy.

David assumed, then, that he might be safe from Saul within the walls of Keilah—the town he had helped to save—but he received word from God that the people he had just risked his neck to help were going to betray him! So David was forced to escape again and try to make up for lost time.

How do you respond when people you've helped are hateful in return? Did you stand up for a friend who was being criticized or bullied? Then when you were under attack and needed a friend, he turned on you? Maybe you went out of your way to be kind to someone, only to find out she's been gossiping about you behind your back. Have you ever made a big sacrifice to help out a friend, and your thoughtfulness was never even acknowledged?

When David faced times like these, he just moved on. He didn't waste valuable time fretting over the ingratitude of others, trusting that God knew the real story.

## WHAT DOES IT TAKE NOT TO CRY FOUL BUT TO LET GOD DEAL WITH THOSE WHO'VE MISTREATED YOU?

### READ UP: MARK 14:43–50 • LUKE 6:27–36

# NOT YET

### READ AHEAD: 1 SAMUEL 26:7–11

*Don't destroy him, for who can lift a hand against the Lord's anointed and be blameless?* 1 Samuel 26:9

Don't be too quick to assume an opportunity is from God just because it's in front of you. Christians talk a lot about God opening doors, and indeed he does. But we need to be discerning, because not every open door is from God.

King Saul had made David's life miserable for years. Because of the king's obsession with killing him, David spent his days on the run—his nights, hiding in caves. And all the while, David had to live with the reality that he, not Saul, was supposed to be the king!

Then it came—an incredible opportunity that would solve all of David's problems! There was Saul, asleep and defenseless at his feet!

David's friend, Abishai, immediately assumed that this chance for rightful revenge must be from God. But David knew God better than that. He understood that God would take care of Saul himself . . . in his own time. He realized that God had called Saul to be king and would deal with him in his own way.

So David spared his life. Saul would later get what he deserved, but not because David had taken matters into his own hands.

We, too, must distinguish between temptation and opportunity. What seems to make perfect sense to us may be totally contrary to God's will. How can we know the difference? We must learn to know God's heart as David did, and God will give us the ability to discern the difference.

## WHAT MAKES GOD'S PATTERN OF JUSTICE SO MUCH BETTER THAN OURS?

**READ UP: ROMANS 12:19–21 • HEBREWS 10:30–31**

# WHICH WAY?

### READ AHEAD: 1 SAMUEL 30:1-8

*David asked the Lord: "Should I pursue these raiders? Will I overtake them?"* 1 Samuel 30:8

David lived in dangerous times. One small mistake could cost him his life. So whenever he needed to know what to do, he asked God. He didn't just ask in generalities. His questions were always specific. And God's answers were equally direct.

There's a theory going around that God doesn't have a specific plan for our lives. This teaching suggests that God doesn't guide his people daily, but that he gives us a brain and leaves us to make our own choices.

The problem with this approach is that it totally ignores what the Bible teaches. From Genesis to Revelation, the Scriptures show us that God has always given clear instructions to his people.

When David needed a specific battle plan, God didn't say, "David, you're a soldier. What do you think?" When David wasn't sure where to go next, God didn't say, "David, you know this area like the back of your hand. Just do what makes sense to you." No, God told him exactly what to do. And when David obeyed, he experienced success.

Don't assume that God isn't interested in the everyday decisions of your life. Yes, he gave you a brain. But he also gave you the Holy Spirit, the church, and his written Word. All of these are ways he communicates with you. He is vitally interested in the details of your life. Never hesitate to seek his direction in any decision.

## WHY IS THE CERTAINTY OF GOD'S DIRECTION SO HARD FOR US TO BELIEVE?

### READ UP: PROVERBS 3:5-6 • JEREMIAH 42:1-3

# EVERYBODY SING!

### READ AHEAD: 2 SAMUEL 6:12-22

*I will celebrate before the Lord, and I will humble myself even more.* 2 Samuel 6:21-22

There's one thing you have to say about David: he wasn't ashamed to worship God!

When David brought back the ark of the covenant to Jerusalem, he was so joyful that he shed his kingly robes and danced all the way down Main Street! Every person in the nation, from the youngest to the oldest, could see David praising God with all of his might! His public display of exuberance so embarrassed his wife (who thought a king ought to show more dignity than that), she mocked him for revealing his emotions so openly.

But David knew he was king only because God had made him king. He was under no delusions of his own importance. He understood that, compared to the King of the universe, he was small potatoes! David loved God so much, and he expressed this love by the way he praised him.

Do you ever find it embarrassing to worship? Do you feel awkward singing in church? Are you afraid to pray publicly? Do you dread being asked to share your salvation experience with a group of people? Are you embarrassed for others to see how deeply you feel about God?

Take courage from David's example. He wasn't ashamed for anyone to see that he loved God. His only concern was that his behavior be pleasing to his King. When you love God with all your heart, you won't be hindered by what anyone else thinks.

## WHAT MUST GOD THINK ABOUT WORSHIP THAT'S FORCED, FAKED, OR FEARED?

**READ UP: PSALM 86:8-12 • PSALM 150:1-6**

# WRONG PLACE, WRONG TIME

**READ AHEAD: 2 SAMUEL 11:1–5**

*In the spring when kings march out to war . . . David remained in Jerusalem.* 2 Samuel 11:1

David learned the hard way that idleness can bring about dangerous temptations.

Kings traditionally led their armies into battle. The Bible doesn't tell us why David chose to stay home this time when he should have been out leading his army. For whatever reason, though, he sent someone else in his place while he remained at home with little to do.

If only he had been where he should have been—doing his job—he wouldn't have come across Bathsheba and committed the sin that would tear apart both their families. David, a man who loved God with all his heart, ended up doing something he would regret for the rest of his life.

You can learn from David's tragic mistake. No matter how strong you think your faith is, you are just as vulnerable as David was. If David could commit a horrible sin, so can you. If you find yourself drifting away from the things you know you should be doing—like Bible study, worship, and prayer—you are placing yourself in great danger.

You will always fill your time by doing something. And if you neglect your Christian life, you'll be tempted to fill the gaps with activities that could bring you enormous heartache. It's far better to be where you're supposed to be than to sit there doing nothing while becoming an easy target for temptation. Begin today to do the things you know you should be doing. It'll save you a lot of regret in the future.

## WHAT ARE SOME OF THE FIRST SIGNALS THAT YOU'RE DRIFTING AWAY SPIRITUALLY?

**READ UP: JEREMIAH 2:1–8 • REVELATION 2:2–5**

# MY BAD

### READ AHEAD: 2 SAMUEL 12:1–10

*Why then have you despised the command of the Lord by doing what I consider evil?* 2 Samuel 12:9

We Christians have lots of pet expressions to describe our sin. We call it backsliding, a bad habit, an error in judgment, or a moment of weakness. Sometimes we just don't want to face up to what we've done at all! But God always calls sin what it is—sin.

When David sinned by committing adultery with Uriah's wife, Bathsheba, God saw David's sin much differently than David did. Rather than repenting immediately, David tried to cover it up by having Uriah killed. Perhaps he thought God would let him get away with this one, since he'd been faithful in so many other ways in the past.

But God wouldn't overlook David's sin. Even though David had been obedient time after time, his sin was an insult to God. David knew better. He knew what God thought about adultery—and about murder—yet he chose to satisfy his own selfish purposes.

We sometimes excuse ourselves for disobeying God's Word. We may assume God will just forgive us and treat us as if it never happened. We may think our disobedience is not a big deal. We may rationalize it by telling ourselves, "Hey, nobody's perfect!"

Perhaps if we really understood how God looks at our sin, we would take his Word far more seriously. Perhaps if we realized that we insult God and his Word every time we sin, we would be more hesitant to do what we know is wrong.

## HOW SERIOUSLY DO YOU AND YOUR FRIENDS TAKE THE SIN IN YOUR LIVES?

**READ UP: PSALM 51:1–13 • PSALM 139:23–24**

# FIRST LINE OF DEFENSE

### READ AHEAD: 2 SAMUEL 22:1–4

*I called to the Lord, who is worthy of praise, and I was saved from my enemies.* 2 Samuel 22:4

People were not always kind to David. They mistrusted and betrayed him. They lied about him and plotted against him. By rights he should have enjoyed a carefree youth, but instead he spent years hiding from a jealous man who was obsessed with murdering him. Where could he turn? Even his wife mocked him!

David had only two choices: he could get angry and blame God for his troubles, or he could find refuge in his relationship with God.

David chose the latter. So the more he suffered, the more he turned to God. And because God was all he had, David discovered God was all he really needed. The Lord became the one constant in David's life, the only one he could really trust, his sure and certain shelter.

David had seen many fortresses in his day. He had even hidden in a few! But none could offer the safety he found in God. As long as David was close to God, he knew he was secure.

You'll experience betrayal in your life. People will misjudge you, let you down, and make attacks against you. It's good to understand, therefore, that your security doesn't come from people but from God.

If you're hurting because you've been treated unfairly, don't turn away from God. Now is the time you need him most. Allow him to be for you all that he was for David. There is no safer place in all the world than in God's hands.

## WHAT ARE SOME STRONG, POWERFUL WORDS YOU COULD USE TO DESCRIBE GOD?

### READ UP: PSALM 89:8–18 • ISAIAH 35:3–10

# WHO AM I?

**READ AHEAD: PSALM 8:3-9**

*What is man that You remember him, the son of man that You look after him?* Psalm 8:4

When David gazed into the starry nighttime sky, he was admiring the same beauty we enjoy now centuries later. He was so moved, in fact, by the enormity of creation that he wrote this psalm as a praise song to its awesome Creator.

Yet David had no idea just how vast the heavens really are! He had no knowledge of galaxies beyond his own. He knew nothing of black holes or light years or supernovas. But what David saw with his own eyes was more than enough to convince him that God is amazing—and that David was very small by comparison.

Yes, reflecting on God's greatness made David keenly aware of his own weakness. Looking at the stars in the sky helped him put his own importance into perspective. It astounded him (as it should astound us) that a being as powerful as God would bother with mere creatures like us. Even more incredible is that God would choose to crown us "with glory and honor" (verse 5).

We still have much to learn about the cosmos, but we know a lot more about it than David did. Therefore, we have even *more* reason to be impressed! So take a walk this evening and study the night sky. And remember this: the same God who put every star in its place wants to have a close, loving relationship with you. Mind-boggling, isn't it?

**DOES GOD WANT US TO FEEL SPECIAL? OR DOES HE WANT US TO FEEL SMALL? OR BOTH?**

**READ UP: JOB 42:1-6 • JOHN 14:1-3**

# THE PLACE OF HONOR

**READ AHEAD: PSALM 16:5–11**

*I keep the Lord in mind always. Because He is at my right hand, I will not be shaken.* Psalm 16:8

At any banquet or formal meal in early Near Eastern culture, a person's closest friend and advisor usually sat on his right-hand side (thus the term "right-hand man"). The Bible refers to Jesus, you may remember, as sitting down after his resurrection "at the right hand of the Majesty on high" (Hebrews 1:3). His Father was giving him the highest honor that exists in heaven or on earth.

Therefore, when David acknowledged God's place at his "right hand," he said a lot in a small phrase. He revealed that God occupied the most important position in his life. He declared that God had priority over *everyone* and *everything*. He called God his close friend and trusted advisor.

David knew from experience that he would be nowhere without God's protection and guidance. For David, there was no question about where to put his trust. As long as God had his rightful place in David's life, David could take on anything the world had to offer. Come what may, he would not be afraid.

Are you aware that you can live with the same confidence David did? Have you reserved the most important place in your life for God, or have you given the honor seat to someone (or something) else?

Only one guest is to sit at your right hand. If you haven't extended this honor to God, now is the time to do so.

## HOW DO YOU TREAT THE PEOPLE YOU TRULY ESTEEM THE HIGHEST?

**READ UP: MATTHEW 21:8–11 • REVELATION 5:11–14**

# TRUST HIM ANYWAY

**READ AHEAD: PSALM 18:30-36**

*God—His way is perfect; the word of the Lord is pure. He is a shield to all who take refuge in Him.* Psalm 18:30

Have you ever wondered if God really knows what he's doing? Sure, you know in your head that God is in control. After all, that's what your Sunday school teachers tell you. Your pastor preaches about it all the time. You've even read it for yourself in the Bible. Yet aren't there times when—deep down—you suspect that God has forgotten you or missed a few important details?

David certainly must have had a few doubts hidden in his heart. God promised that David would be king, yet he seemed to have overlooked a significant obstacle—Saul—who continued to remain on the throne for years afterward.

Where was God when David had to flee to the hills to escape Saul's sword? Didn't God care that David was forced to live in caves, or that he once had to fake insanity just to preserve his life?

If David did wonder about the reliability of God's word, he came to understand that his doubts were groundless. Through experience David learned that God was indeed aware of every detail in his life. Even in the cold, damp caves, God was there. David discovered that he didn't have to understand God's ways in order to trust him.

You shouldn't be afraid to trust God either, even when you can't figure out what he's doing. You don't have to know everything about him in order to find refuge in him.

**WHAT WOULD YOU SAY TO SOMEONE WHO THINKS YOU'RE NUTS TO TRUST IN GOD?**

**READ UP: ISAIAH 50:7-10 • JOHN 9:24-25**

# FAITHFUL AND TRUE

### READ AHEAD: PSALM 25:8–10

*All the Lord's ways show faithful love and truth to those who keep His covenant and decrees.* Psalm 25:10

At times you may be tempted to think God asks too much of you. You might feel as though he expects you to be perfect and doesn't want you to have any fun. If this is how you view God, you need to get to know him better!

Through a variety of experiences, David grew to know God well . . . and concluded that God always relates to his people lovingly and faithfully. No matter what his circumstances were, David found that God was not only there for him but also knew what was best for him. Even God's most demanding commandments were merely another way of expressing his love for us. Although there were times when life seemed hopeless for David, God fulfilled every promise he made to him.

If you look at your own situation and doubt that God loves you, or if you question his willingness to keep his promises to you, remember David's words. The longer you walk with God, the more clearly you'll see that everything he does in your life is done in perfect love. Even when he disciplines you or puts restrictions on you, it's because he loves you so much.

God's faithfulness to you is beyond question. But what about your faithfulness to him? Will God find you to be as faithful to him as he is to you? If you will trust him and keep his ways, you'll experience his faithfulness and enjoy the results.

## WHEN (IF EVER) DO YOU FIND YOURSELF DOUBTING GOD'S FAITHFULNESS?

### READ UP: DEUTERONOMY 7:7–11 • 2 THESSALONIANS 3:1–5

# I FEEL BETTER ALREADY

**READ AHEAD: PSALM 32:1-7**

*How happy is the one whose transgression is forgiven, whose sin is covered!* Psalm 32:1

Guilt is a heavy load to carry. When you've done something horrible, and you know it, it really weighs you down. You can only carry unconfessed sin around with you for so long before you grow exhausted from it, wishing for things to be like they were before—before you saddled yourself down with this oppressive burden of shame.

David knew what guilt and shame felt like. His sin sapped his strength the way an unbearably hot summer day drains your energy. He couldn't get his mind off it. He walked around feeling its weight on his back. His guilt was too much for him to handle.

But when he could bear it no more, he confessed his sin to God and sought forgiveness. Immediately, the load was lifted. He felt renewed and energized. He enjoyed a sense of freedom that he hadn't known for a long time.

The irony of unconfessed sin is that God already knows about it anyway. We try to hide it, but there's no hiding it from God. He simply waits for us to acknowledge that we've sinned and to admit we were wrong.

If sin is weighing you down, you're carrying a burden you don't have to bear. Confess your sin to God. Seek his forgiveness. Ask him to restore you so you can enjoy your relationship with him once again. Go ahead. You'll feel like a new person.

## WHAT KEEPS US FROM GOING TO GOD WHEN WE KNOW WE'VE SINNED?

**READ UP: EXODUS 34:6-9 • HEBREWS 4:14-16**

# ANY TIME'S A GOOD TIME

## READ AHEAD: PSALM 34:1–3

*I will praise the Lord at all times; His praise will always be on my lips.* Psalm 34:1

It shouldn't surprise us to read that David wanted to praise God his entire life. After all, it seems he was always writing psalms and singing praises to God.

It's interesting, though, that David wrote the above words immediately after one of the most humiliating experiences of his life. Even while trying to stay one step ahead of his old nemesis, King Saul, David experienced a close call with another enemy: the Philistine king of Gath. The only way out of danger was to fake being insane so his enemy would see no need to kill him.

Talk about a low point! Here was a man destined to be king, ranting and slobbering all over himself to throw the enemy off his scent. Did obeying God really require such a loss of dignity?

This certainly doesn't seem like the time for David to burst into songs of praise, yet that's exactly what he did! He understood that God had again spared his life, and David wanted to praise him right away.

Sometimes, we completely miss something good that God has just done in our lives, choosing to concentrate only on the negatives of the situation. At other times we do see God's goodness, but we're too busy to praise him.

David, however, made it his habit to praise God always, no matter where he was or how he felt. That's not a bad habit for us to copy.

## HOW CAN YOU BEGIN TO MAKE WORSHIP YOUR FIRST RESPONSE TO EVERYTHING?

## READ UP: ROMANS 11:33–36 • REVELATION 15:1–4

# FEAR NOT

### READ AHEAD: PSALM 34:4–7

*I sought the Lord, and He answered me and delivered me from all my fears.* Psalm 34:4

People can be afraid of almost anything.
- There's *agoraphobia*—the fear of public places.
- *Claustrophobia*—the fear of closed-in spaces.
- *Astraphobia*—fear of thunder.
- *Algophobia*—fear of pain.
- *Hydrophobia*—fear of water.
- *Pyrophobia*—fear of fire.

And those who don't suffer from any of these phobias have a number of other fears to choose from. Some people are terrified of failure, so they never attempt anything. Others are afraid of what others think, so they withdraw into their own little world where life feels safer. Some folks would rather bathe in battery acid than give a speech. And just about everybody at some point in their lives is afraid of death and disease.

We all know what fear feels like. It can consume us, causing us to do irrational things, crippling us emotionally so we no longer enjoy life the way God planned.

But it doesn't have to be this way. God wants to deliver us from our fears and give us back the joy that fear takes away. David had lots of reasons for fear, but he took them all to God. And to his delight, God "delivered" him from every single one!

## WHAT'S HAPPENED IN THE PAST WHEN YOU'VE TAKEN YOUR FEARS TO GOD?

### READ UP: NUMBERS 21:33–35 • LUKE 1:68–75

# GOD IS GOOD

**READ AHEAD: PSALM 34:8–10**

*Taste and see that the Lord is good. How happy is the man who takes refuge in Him.* Psalm 34:8

God loves you more than anyone else can love you, and he has some wonderful plans tailor-made for your life. He's reserving a place in heaven for you that's indescribably exquisite.

It's impossible to understand just how good God really is.

Some people, though, never come to know God as he is. They maintain a mental image of him that's totally distorted from reality. Some see him as a heartless being who delights in condemning people to hell. Others consider him a cruel puppeteer, engineering natural disasters at whim.

Many people don't view God in such a drastic way, but their view is distorted nonetheless. They may think of him as a legalistic ruler who puts restrictions on everyone and everything. Many people don't know what God is really like because they don't even acknowledge his existence. They simply consider him a nonentity.

Saddest of all, many *Christians* don't really know what God is like. They view him warily, from a distance, as though he's just waiting for them to mess up so he can punish them. All of these are false images of God . . . because God is good!

But no one can tell you how good God is. You have to experience him for yourself to get the best view. God wants you to get to know him, to spend time discovering what he's really like. So come in a little deeper, and be delighted to discover just how wonderful he really is!

## HOW HAS GOD SHOWN HIS ABSOLUTE GOODNESS TO YOU?

**READ UP: DEUTERONOMY 26:1–11 • MARK 10:17–18**

# ENJOYING GOD

**READ AHEAD: PSALM 37:3–6**

*Take delight in the Lord, and He will give you your heart's desires.*
Psalm 37:4

People often think of God only in terms of the Ten Commandments: he lays down the rules, and we wear ourselves out trying to follow them.

Even some Christians view God as little more than a cosmic policeman whose job is to catch us breaking the law—while our job is to avoid getting caught!

If that's so, we are sadly deceived. The truth is, knowing God is the most freeing experience we could ever have. Spending time with him each day ought to be a delight.

Sometimes we get things backwards in our thinking. We act like spoiled children, seeking the Father only when we want something. We throw tantrums when he doesn't meet our demands, concluding that he must not love us. But the problem isn't with God. It's with us! God *delights* in our company. He takes pleasure in answering our prayers.

The more time we spend getting to know God, the more we'll see just how much he loves us. We'll grow to understand the difference between selfish whims and true prayer. We'll find ourselves praying the way God desires us to pray, shrinking the distance between what we want and what God wants.

So if your prayers seem to be going unanswered, pay attention to the way you're praying. Are you reciting a wish list, or are you getting to know God? Knowing him is far more important than getting what you want.

## WHY WOULD IT SURPRISE MOST PEOPLE TO KNOW THAT CHRISTIANITY IS ENJOYABLE?

**READ UP: ISAIAH 61:10–11 • ZEPHANIAH 3:14–17**

# NEVER FORSAKEN

### READ AHEAD: PSALM 37:23–29

*I have been young and now I am old, yet I have not seen the righteous abandoned.* Psalm 37:25

David had walked with God for a long time. As a young boy herding sheep, David had played songs of praise on his harp. As a soldier going into battle, he had put his trust in God. When his enemies were trying to destroy him, David had relied on God to save him. When he had needed guidance as king, God had always been there to give it.

But David was an old man now, having trusted God throughout his long life. And as he looked back over all his experiences, he concluded that he had never seen God fail a righteous person. Not once!

So if your heart is right before God, this promise is for you. God has never failed anyone who sought to obey him, and he's not going to start now!

If you're choosing your own way, however, don't hold onto the false assurance that God is obligated to meet your needs. Many Christians are confident that God will take care of them simply because they are believers, even though they continue to live in disobedience. The only ones who can count on God's blessings are those who choose to live a righteous life.

Are you worried about whether God will take care of your needs? If you're living the way God wants, you have no reason to be concerned. God will be just as faithful with you as he was with David . . . and with every other righteous person who ever lived.

## DAVID WASN'T PERFECT BY A LONG SHOT. SO HOW COULD HE MAKE THIS CLAIM FOR HIMSELF?

### READ UP: DEUTERONOMY 31:1–6 • ISAIAH 41:17–20

# MUSIC TO LIVE BY

**READ AHEAD: PSALM 40:1-3**

*He put a new song in my mouth, a hymn of praise to our God.*
Psalm 40:3

At some time or other, anyone can fall into the pit. You know the place—where everything looks dark and gloomy. You feel all alone. Things look hopeless. Every time you try to climb out, you lose the grip on your footing and slide back down. You feel miserable about yourself and about life in general. It seems like no one understands what you're going through . . . and if they did understand, they wouldn't care! The only song in your heart is off-key.

David knew the pit from experience. But he also knew that there was just one way out. So he did the only thing within his power to do: he cried out to God and then waited patiently for his answer.

Sure enough, God rescued him, picking him up and putting him on solid ground, renewing his confidence and restoring his hope. God even gave him a new song—a song of hope and joy instead of bitterness and despair. As hopeless as the pit had seemed to David moments before, now the place had no power over him.

Maybe you're in the pit of despair right now. Perhaps your current situation seems hopeless. You may feel as if no one cares. Have you called out to God? Wait patiently and trust him. He'll get you out and put you on your feet again. You may be only a prayer away from a heart filled with joy!

## UNDER WHAT CIRCUMSTANCES COULD IT BE GOD'S WILL FOR YOU TO BE IN THE PIT?

**READ UP: JONAH 2:1-10 • LUKE 18:35-43**

# IN BROAD DAYLIGHT

### READ AHEAD: 2 SAMUEL 12:11–14

*You acted in secret, but I will do this before all Israel and in broad daylight.* 2 Samuel 12:12

Most of us want our good deeds to be made public and our sins to be kept private. Sin by its very nature is shrouded in darkness.

When David sinned by taking another man's wife as his own, he went to great lengths to cover up his actions. He even had the woman's husband murdered so he wouldn't have to face him! He used all his powers as king to escape the consequences of his sin.

We may marvel at David's foolishness in trying to conceal his crimes of adultery and murder. But are we any smarter? How often do we do things in secret that we never expect to be made public? How often do we see people in the news who are humiliated when their private lives are opened up for public viewing? They never dreamed their secrets would come to light and bring them and their families such grief and embarrassment.

David was the most powerful person in Israel, yet even he couldn't escape God's scrutiny when he sinned. So we're only fooling ourselves if we think we can sin and never be found out. The only way to live without fear of being exposed is to live a clean life.

So don't be as ignorant as David and countless other red-faced sinners have been. The things you do in secret not only *can* but most likely *will* be proclaimed in broad daylight. Be sure it's something you don't mind the world knowing.

## WHAT WOULD BE GOD'S PURPOSE IN EXPOSING A PERSON'S SINFUL SECRETS?

### READ UP: JOB 24:13–17 • ROMANS 13:11–14

# WHAT BIG LESSONS CAN YOU LEARN FROM DAVID'S LIFE?

# THE FAITH WORKOUT

Many Bible scholars believe that James—the writer of the New Testament letter that bears his name—was actually the half brother of Jesus. Did you know that? But whether he was or wasn't, he certainly knew Jesus well.

The book of James is a treasure chest of practical, down-to-earth wisdom. He gets right to the heart of what it truly means to be Christ's disciple, stripping away everything about the Christian life that's false and pretentious, leaving no doubt about how Christians should live.

The flavor of the book of James is characterized by this verse: "Be doers of the word and not hearers only" (1:22). To anyone who wants a long, drawn-out discussion on how to approach the Scriptures, James in essence wrote, "Just do what it says." That's the way James put things. Directly. Clearly. He tackled all the big subjects—like obedience, temptation, wisdom, faithfulness, sin, and more—in a straightforward, precise way that left no question about what he was trying to say!

All of this comes together to make James's letter a fascinating, easy-to-understand guide to living out your faith day by day. It's a short book—only five chapters. So over the next fifteen days of devotions, we'll be able to cover much of what James had to say. But be sure to take time to read the verses we don't cover, because the entire book is filled with practical, relevant advice that'll help you know how to live a happy, victorious Christian life.

Ready to hear it straight up, with no nonsense? That's how faith really works!

# A BAD CASE OF JOY

### READ AHEAD: JAMES 1:2–4

*Consider it a great joy, my brothers, whenever you experience various trials.* James 1:2

When we go through tough times, we experience a variety of emotions, but joy usually isn't one of them. When trials come, we become frustrated that things aren't going the way we'd like. We get angry at others, God, and ourselves.

Yet according to James, we are not at the mercy of our circumstances. Incredibly, in fact, James said we should "consider it a great joy" when we go through adversity. This forces us to ask, "What could be good about hard times?"

For one thing, James said that when our faith is tested, we learn to rely on God. If we never experienced difficulties, we'd never learn to trust God the way we should. That's because tough times build endurance. They're like an exercise routine, which causes us a measure of discomfort but also strengthens our bodies.

Yes, misfortune can be painful, but it can also make you a stronger Christian. When God carries you through a dark period, you gain a fresh understanding of how much he loves you. Your faith is made stronger, and you're more prepared to trust him the next time. It isn't that you *enjoy* suffering, but you can find joy in knowing that God will bring about good through the worst situations.

So if things look gloomy for you right now, take heart. Allow God the opportunity to care for you and strengthen you. He alone can give you joy that no circumstance can take away.

## HOW HAS SOMEONE INSPIRED YOU BY LIVING OUT THIS ILLOGICAL ADVICE?

### READ UP: 2 TIMOTHY 1:8–12 • HEBREWS 10:32–39

# WISE CHOICE

**READ AHEAD: JAMES 1:5–8**

*If any of you lacks wisdom, he should ask God, who gives to all generously and without criticizing.* James 1:5

If there's anything required for us in order to get along successfully in this world, it's wisdom. We can be fabulously wealthy, unbelievably good-looking, incredibly intelligent, and amazingly talented. But without wisdom we'll make one stupid choice after another—some that could ruin us!

We confront new problems and decisions every day. We deal with all kinds of people and situations. One wrong decision in any of these areas can hurt us for the rest of our lives. That's why the Bible is filled with warnings for the foolish person. Life is simply too complicated to be self-centered and short-sighted. We all need wisdom.

Wisdom is different from knowledge. You can read thousands of books, earn a dozen degrees, and take a hundred classes to acquire knowledge. But wisdom comes only from God.

Wisdom is the ability to apply what you know to how you live. It means making decisions by understanding which option is from God and which ones are from the world. It's having the insight to know when a relationship is so unhealthy it needs to be broken off. It's being able to take what you read in the Bible and apply it to your circumstances.

You don't learn wisdom. It's a gift that God wants to *give* you. So every morning, before you face what the day holds, ask God for the wisdom to guide you through. James assures you that God will give it to you generously.

## HOW CAN PEOPLE BE REALLY, REALLY SMART AND STILL MAKE SUCH REALLY BAD DECISIONS?

**READ UP: PROVERBS 2:1–10 • 1 CORINTHIANS 3:18–23**

# THE SOURCE

## READ AHEAD: JAMES 1:16–18

*Every generous act and every perfect gift is from above, coming down from the Father of lights.* James 1:17

One of Satan's tricks is trying to convince us that we don't need God, that we can get along fine without him, that the good things in our lives are the result of our own hard work or good luck.

James agreed with this by warning us that we're in dangerous territory if we ever start to believe that we're responsible for what we have. God, who gave us life itself, is the one who's behind everything in our lives that's worthwhile.

We often neglect to notice gifts from God. When we're short of money, for example, and then unexpectedly receive a check that exactly matches our need, we exclaim, "What luck! I can't believe how fortunate I am to receive this money—right when I needed it most!"

Or perhaps when we're feeling discouraged and a friend suddenly shows up to encourage us, we say, "What a coincidence that this person would come along at that very moment!" Too often we don't make the connection between the good things that happen in our lives and God's provision for us.

Take some time to consider all the good things that have crossed your path recently. Review some of the blessings you've asked God to provide for you. Then begin writing down your prayer requests so you can take notice when God answers them. Make the link between the many blessings in your life and the one who deserves the thanks!

## WHAT ABOUT THE THINGS WE WORK FOR AND EARN? WHO GIVES US THOSE?

## READ UP: DEUTERONOMY 28:7–13 • PSALM 67:6–7

# JUST DO IT

**READ AHEAD: JAMES 1:22–25**

*Be doers of the word and not hearers only, deceiving yourselves.*
James 1:22

James warned us about something we're probably all a little guilty of: substituting good intentions for real deeds, making big promises instead of actually delivering the goods.

We often spend our time going to church, attending Bible studies, reading Christian books and magazines, and listening to Christian music. We may think that in doing these things we're living the Christian life. But we may be deceiving ourselves! Though all of these activities are worthy pursuits, they're all for nothing if we never put into practice the knowledge we gain from them.

Our generation has access to more biblical information than any in the past, yet we're not necessarily the most skilled at living it out. Many times what we need is not another conference to go to or another sermon to hear. We simply need to put into practice what we've already learned.

Just knowing the right things to do is not the same as doing them, and promising to act on them is not the same thing as putting them into practice. God is not interested in our knowledge or our intentions. He's interested in our obedience.

Consider today if there's anything you know God wants you to do that you've been putting off until you gain more knowledge. Then be a doer of his word, not just a listener.

**WHAT CLUTTERS YOUR PATH BETWEEN HEARTFELT PROMISES AND ACTUAL OBEDIENCE?**

**READ UP: ISAIAH 1:18–20 • LUKE 8:11–15**

# SPIRITUAL SPOILERS

### READ AHEAD: JAMES 1:26–27

*If anyone thinks he is religious, without controlling his tongue but deceiving his heart, his religion is useless.* James 1:26

James, in his typically straightforward way, warned about living under false assumptions. He understood how easy it is to become self-satisfied in the way we're living, when in reality there are some things that need to change radically.

Here, James referred to the destructive power of our words, saying to us that we can discredit everything we claim to believe by not controlling our language.

The tongue, according to James, is "a world of unrighteousness . . . a restless evil, full of deadly poison" (James 3:6, 8). This may sound pretty grim. But we know it only takes one ugly comment to devastate a friend. An angry outburst can destroy a relationship and betray a trust.

So you can talk all you want about your Christian faith, but if you're known as a liar, a gossip, or a betrayer, your reputation will drown out your Christian witness. In your heart you may genuinely care about others, but your inability to control your tongue will negate your good intentions.

There *is* a positive spin on James's warning: the words we say also have the potential for much good. Our words can encourage someone who's down, challenge others to grow in their faith, share the good news of Christ, and praise God. The important thing is never to let our guard down when it comes to what we say, because just as we can use our words to build up our Christian witness, we can also tear it down.

## HOW HARD IS IT TO FORGET A CUTTING REMARK SOMEONE MAKES ABOUT YOU?

### READ UP: JOB 16:1–5 • 1 PETER 3:8–12

# SAY IT LIKE YOU MEAN IT

**READ AHEAD: JAMES 2:14–17**

*[If] one of you says to them, "Go in peace, keep warm, and eat well" . . . what good is it?* James 2:16

Suppose you were going through a really difficult time, and everybody knew it. A friend approached you and said, "Hey, I sure do hope things get better for you. Call me if you need anything." Then he or she hurried off to an appointment.

A second friend came along, listened to you talk about your troubles, and said, "I know I can't make all your problems go away, but let's go get some dinner and see what we can do about it."

Obviously, you'd prefer the offer of the second friend over the first, even though both of them wished you well.

James said Christianity is like that. Faith is much more than just saying the right words. Words are cheap. They cost us nothing but our breath. Deeds cost a lot more.

We can become pleased with ourselves when we're learning so much about faith in our Bible study. But if the time comes to trust God and we refuse him, our faith is no more real than it was before. Christianity is not just an academic pursuit. It applies to everyday real life.

Is there someone close to you who needs more than just your words of comfort? Is there something you can do that'll cost you something but will meet a real need? If you show your faith by your actions—not just your words—both you and the one you help will receive the blessing.

## WHAT WOULD GENUINE CONCERN FOR SOMEONE REALLY COST YOU?

**READ UP: MATTHEW 15:3–9 • 1 THESSALONIANS 2:7–8**

# ALL IN YOUR HEAD?

**READ AHEAD: JAMES 2:18–20**

*You believe that God is one; you do well. The demons also believe—and they shudder.* James 2:19

Demons have pretty solid theology. They believe in God's existence. They also believe that God sent his Son to the cross to die for the sins of humanity. Why wouldn't they believe? They were there, fighting God's plan every step of the way. They were there to witness Christ's resurrection from the dead and his triumphant return to heaven.

They believe all the right things. They know certain facts to be true. For example, they know Jesus is powerful, because they experienced his mighty strength firsthand every time he cast some of their number out of demon-possessed people. But this knowledge doesn't lead them to *trust* in Jesus' power. Their theology has no impact on their behavior. Their belief doesn't cause them to do anything about it.

Obviously, claiming to "believe" is not the same thing as faith; otherwise, the demons would be pleasing to God. The way to tell if someone trusts God is not whether she knows God is trustworthy—or even whether she *says* God can be trusted. It's whether or not she actually trusts in God.

Examine your own life. Are you living under the assumption that your knowledge or even your words are evidence of your faith? Don't be fooled. What you really believe about God will be proven by what you do. It doesn't matter how many times you say "Jesus is Lord" to someone. What you really believe is shown by your actions.

## WHAT WOULD BE DIFFERENT ABOUT CHRISTIANITY IF IT WAS NOTHING MORE THAN HEAD KNOWLEDGE?

**READ UP: JOHN 8:42–47 • HEBREWS 11:1–6**

# PRAYER POSTURING

**READ AHEAD: JAMES 4:1–3**

*You ask and don't receive because you act wrongly, so that you may spend it on your desires for pleasure.* James 4:3

Is there such a thing as a bad prayer? Isn't God pleased with *any* prayer we offer him, just so long as we take time to pray?

No. God doesn't see all prayers in the same light. Instead, he looks beyond the words we say to the condition of our hearts.

James addressed a group of believers who were apparently becoming frustrated because they weren't getting what they asked for . . . and were beginning to doubt if prayer really worked at all.

But James pointed out the selfish motives behind their prayers—prayers that consisted of long lists of things they wanted for themselves. Like spoiled children at Christmas, they would go before God with their wish lists, watching impatiently for the parcels to arrive. James made it clear—this isn't real prayer. God does not reward selfishness.

One of the biggest benefits of praying is that it takes our attention away from ourselves and causes us to think more about others. It makes us seek God's will above our own. Only then are our prayers pleasing to God and worthy of his answer.

If you've been disappointed in the way God's been answering your prayers, perhaps it's time to examine the motives behind what you pray. When God is your main focus in prayer, you'll receive all the things he desires for you.

## HOW DO YOU CHECK YOUR OWN PRAYER MOTIVES?

**READ UP: LUKE 18:1–8 • 1 JOHN 5:14–15**

# UP CLOSE

### READ AHEAD: JAMES 4:4–8

*Draw near to God, and He will draw near to you.*
James 4:8

Do you sometimes feel as though God is right there with you, while at other times he seems thousands of miles away? When you pray, do you sometimes feel close to God, but at other times you're not even sure he's listening? Jesus promised that he would never leave us, so why are there times when we don't sense his presence?

James gave us the answer to these questions in our verse for today. When we're separated from God, we're the ones who have strayed, not him. There may be sin in our lives that we need to confess. Or we may be so distracted by other things that we've neglected to spend time in prayer and Bible study.

When we realize this has happened, we should immediately seek God with all our strength . . . and *keep* seeking him until we once again enjoy close fellowship with him.

If your relationship with God is cold and distant, examine your life to see if there are any sins or attitudes you need to ask God to remove. Spend time in prayer and in his Word. Go to him with a humble heart and confess your sin.

Always remember, God is not the one who changes. We are the ones who wander, and it's our responsibility to return to him. He stands ready to love us, forgive us, and restore our relationship.

## WHAT'S KEPT YOU AT A DISTANCE FROM GOD BEFORE? WHAT'S BROUGHT YOU CLOSER?

### READ UP: PSALM 73:21–28 • ZEPHANIAH 3:1–5

# THE QUICKEST WAY UP

**READ AHEAD: JAMES 4:9–10**

*Humble yourselves before the Lord, and He will exalt you.*
James 4:10

Humility doesn't come naturally to most of us. We may consider ourselves quite modest, yet it's amazing how quickly we can become proud of what we've done. We want people to admire us and envy us because of our talents and our accomplishments.

The Bible, though, warns us that we're setting ourselves up for disappointment when we exaggerate our own importance, because in doing so we lose sight of our dependence on God. This kind of pride has caused the downfall of many a person, going back to the very beginning of time.

The only defense against pride is humility. That's why James urged us to keep ourselves in proper perspective. When we remember that we owe everything to God, it's hard to grow arrogant. That's not to say we consider ourselves worthless. On the contrary, we are highly valuable to God, who paid for our salvation at an incredible price. But we must remember that we are treasured because of who God is, not because of anything we've done on our own.

How much better for us to choose humility—because just as God promises to "exalt" the humble, he also promises that those who exalt themselves will be humbled! So the choice is ours. We can seek to build ourselves up before others (only to be brought back down), or we can humble ourselves and allow God to honor us.

## HOW DO YOU GENERALLY HANDLE A COMPLIMENT?

**READ UP: PSALM 84:10–12 • JOHN 15:5–8**

# NOT SO GOOD

**READ AHEAD: JAMES 4:13–17**

*For the person who knows to do good and doesn't do it, it is a sin.*
James 4:17

When we talk about sin, we usually refer to the bad things people do—like lying, stealing, cussing, and killing. We sometimes forget that we can also sin by the things we *don't* do.

These are called sins of *omission*—sins we commit by failing to do what we should—and though they are much more subtle, they are just as harmful. Sin is not just doing the wrong things; it also includes *not* doing the *right* things.

God will lead you, for example, to share your faith, help someone in need, or forgive someone who's hurt you. If you don't, you're sinning. If you *delay*, you are sinning. You may assume that you're living a blameless life because you don't steal, lie, or cheat others. But if you've been neglecting to do the things you know God has told you to do, you've sinned just the same.

It's easy for us to see the harm done by raw, blatant sins like gossip, stealing, or murder. These result in everything from hurt feelings to loss of property or even loss of life. But the damage can be just as severe (even though a lot less obvious) when we harm others by not responding when God prompts us to get involved where he is at work.

We'll never know (this side of heaven) all the ways our obedience has benefited someone else. But we know this: when we refuse to obey God, we rob others and ourselves of God's blessing.

**WHAT ARE SOME THINGS GOD'S BEEN LEADING YOU TO DO BUT YOU HAVEN'T BEEN DOING?**

**READ UP: MATTHEW 25:41–45 • LUKE 11:39–42**

# KEEP IT SHORT

**READ AHEAD: JAMES 5:7–12**

*Your "yes" must be "yes," and your "no" must be "no," so that you won't fall under judgment.* James 5:12

How reliable are you? When you give your word, do others consider it as good as done? When you make a vow, do your friends take you seriously, or do they laughingly dismiss your words as yet another empty promise?

Your word is a great indicator of your character. If people don't take what you say seriously, you probably have an untrustworthy disposition.

In James's day, just as in ours, people wanted respect. They wanted to be listened to. So when these people gave their opinion, they were likely to add, "I swear by heaven it is so!" or something to that effect. (Today, someone might say, "As God is my witness.") They thought that if they brought the weight of heaven to bear on their statements, it would give their words more credibility.

James said, however, that your word ought to be enough. If you have to back up what you say with swear words and extra witnesses, then your own reputation isn't worth much.

So again: How seriously do people take you when you tell them something? Does your life back up what you say?

If you always keep your word, people will learn to trust you. You don't have to swear by *anything* when you consistently tell the truth. On the other hand, if you make promises but then forget to keep them, you may need to rebuild your reputation.

## HOW IMPORTANT DO YOU THINK THIS ISSUE WILL BE LONG-TERM IN YOUR LIFE?

**READ UP: PROVERBS 10:19–21 • ECCLESIASTES 5:2–7**

# OUT IN THE OPEN

**READ AHEAD: JAMES 5:13–16**

*Confess your sins to one another and pray for one another, so that you may be healed.* James 5:16

One of the healthiest things Christians can do is confess their sins, both to God and to fellow believers. If we act as if we never sin, we fool no one but ourselves.

When we sin against God, he wants us to admit our fault and seek his forgiveness. And when we offend another person, James urged us to go to that person and try to restore the broken relationship.

Sin that isn't dealt with doesn't just go away. Until we confess it, it stays with us and eats at our soul. It's not always easy to do—to admit we've acted badly and have done things we're not proud of—but the relief that comes as a result makes it worth the effort.

The healing begins within our own heart. We start to feel as if a heavy burden has been lifted off us. We're then free to approach God with a clean heart, which makes our relationship with him grow stronger. Even if the one we've offended refuses to forgive us, we're freed from the guilt of the unconfessed sin that weighed us down.

Our responsibility, of course, doesn't end with mere confession. The next step is to change our sinful behavior. We must truly learn from our mistake and strive never to commit that same sin again. If someone still has something against us, we should keep trying to mend the broken relationship. But it all begins with confession and prayer.

## WHAT HAPPENS TO PEOPLE WHO NEVER GATHER ENOUGH COURAGE TO CONFESS?

**READ UP: NEHEMIAH 1:4–9 • 1 JOHN 1:5–10**

# JOE ORDINARY

**READ AHEAD: JAMES 5:17–18**

*Elijah was a man with a nature like ours.* James 5:17

Sometimes we're tempted to think, "If only I were a spiritual giant, like my pastor, or my grandmother, or the people in the Bible, then my prayers would be answered like theirs!" We assume we're too ordinary to see extraordinary things happen when we pray.

James gave a very pointed challenge to that line of thought.

He reminded us that Elijah, a man who saw God perform incredible miracles through his life, was just an ordinary guy. He had fears and doubts and mood swings like we do. He had moments when he stood up bravely for God, and he had other times when he ran for his life!

Yet despite Elijah's weaknesses, God chose to answer his prayers in miraculous, spectacular ways.

Elijah was no super saint. He didn't have a built-in ability to trust God or to make miracles happen. He was just a normal person praying for God's will to be done.

Anyone can have faith. It's not based on intelligence or ability but on our willingness to trust what God says. It means accepting that the promises God gives us in the Bible are true.

So don't be afraid to trust him out of fear that he won't answer the prayers of an ordinary person. You, too, can see God do great things through your prayers . . . just like Elijah did! When you pray within God's will, the ordinary becomes extraordinary!

## WHERE DOES THIS SPIRITUAL INFERIORITY COMPLEX COME FROM?

**READ UP: JEREMIAH 9:23–24 • JOHN 14:12–14**

# EXCUSE ME

**READ AHEAD: JAMES 5:19-20**

*Whoever turns a sinner from the error of his way will save his life from death and cover a multitude of sins.* James 5:20

We live in a world that teaches us to mind our own business. We try not to get involved in other people's problems. We tell ourselves it's not our place.

But this attitude is completely opposite to what the Bible teaches. As Christians, we are called to become *involved* in the lives of others, especially when we see someone headed for trouble.

Sometimes we're reluctant to say anything to others because we don't want to offend them. We don't want to act "holier than thou." Besides, if we point out a certain sin of theirs, they might point back at us and begin naming *our* sins! Therefore, we often say nothing, and think to ourselves that we've done the most Christian thing we could do.

James argued, however, that when we help someone avoid the danger of sin, we're saving that person from death!

We need to check to see what's happening in the lives of people around us. If our friends keep falling into sin and we keep minding our own business, we have failed them as Christian friends.

Is there someone you need to lovingly warn? Have you spotted something that needs to be mentioned—not in judgment but in genuine love? Take courage, then. Regardless of the response you think you'll receive, speak up before it's too late. Do it because you care about the well-being of your friend.

## HOW WOULD YOU PROBABLY REACT IF SOMEONE CHALLENGED YOU ABOUT A SIN AREA?

**READ UP: JEREMIAH 26:1-6 • EZEKIEL 33:7-11**

# HOW DO YOU LIKE JAMES'S STRAIGHT-TALKING STYLE?

# NEWS YOU CAN USE

Jesus was saddened when he looked out at the needy crowds who followed him. They were like sheep without a shepherd—wandering aimlessly, wasting away, with little to show for all the effort they were putting into life. Jesus knew it was time to send out some help, time to take his kingdom to the streets.

And it would start with twelve of the unlikeliest of men.

Only God knows what Jesus thought when he first looked at the twelve guys the Father had chosen to be Christ's closest group of followers—a tax collector, a few fishermen, a member of a radical political movement . . . and not a preacher among them! It was time, it seemed, for a serious talk.

So Jesus called his men together and gave it to them straight. First, the good news: he would give them the power to heal the sick, drive out demons, and even raise the dead!

Then the not-so-good news: "I'm sending you out like sheep among wolves" (Matthew 10:16), complete with the very real possibility of floggings, arrests, and persecution. Jesus laid it all out for them—the good, the bad, and the scary. He told them exactly what to expect and how to respond. They would encounter a whole lot of incredible experiences, but no surprises.

Jesus' words are here for us, too—captured most completely for us in the Gospel of Matthew—words that are still relevant to us because we, too, are his messengers to a hurting world. So let's give these direct quotes a closer look over the next seventeen readings, and learn about what it means to be a follower of Jesus.

# IN AND OUT

## READ AHEAD: MATTHEW 10:5-10

*You have received free of charge; give free of charge.*
Matthew 10:8

You're probably familiar with the term *oxymoron*—words that don't sound like they go together. Here are a few:

- "Sweet sorrow."
- "Uniquely uniform."
- "Cute in an ugly sort of way."

The term "selfish Christian" is another oxymoron—or at least it *should* be. That's because Christians have already received more than any unbeliever has. Therefore, we have more to give than anyone else does.

We Christians are experts at receiving. We've been given God's love, forgiveness, and healing. We've eagerly accepted eternal life. We've been adopted into God's family, and we gladly claim the myriad promises the Bible says are just for us. We don't pretend to have *earned* any of these things. They're all free gifts from God, and we know it. Nor are we dense enough to suppose we could ever repay God for them.

He does ask one thing, however. He wants us to become experts at giving as well as receiving.

Selfishness is a sign that we've forgotten who we are. If we give only to people we consider worthy of our gift, we've missed the whole point. Whether or not the person in need deserves our help is irrelevant. The evidence of genuine Christianity is the willingness to give whatever it takes to whoever's in need.

## HOW WOULD YOU DESCRIBE THE DIFFERENCE BETWEEN GIVERS AND TAKERS?

**READ UP: DEUTERONOMY 16:16-17 • LUKE 14:12-14**

# HEADS UP

**READ AHEAD: MATTHEW 10:11–17**

*I'm sending you out like sheep among wolves. Therefore be as shrewd as serpents and as harmless as doves.* Matthew 10:16

Do you ever feel like the world is out to get you? *It is!* Some people think Christians are naïve. They see our meekness as a weakness. So they try to take advantage of us, assuming our only option is to turn the other cheek. Or they try to manipulate us into sinning . . . to prove we're no different than they are.

Jesus had two words of advice for us: *Wise up!* Yes, we're supposed to be kind and loving, but we're not to be foolish. We're to be like three types of very different animals: like *sheep*, like *snakes*, and like *doves*.

The *sheep* part we know about. We've read all the biblical analogies that tell us how we're the sheep and Jesus is the Good Shepherd. But as sheep we must understand that there are wolves in the bushes who aren't looking out for our best interests!

That's why Jesus also warned us to be as shrewd as *snakes*. Biblically speaking, snakes are usually the bad guys. But they're also very clever, just as we should be to avoid falling blindly into the traps of cunning, evil people.

But if all this talk makes you feel paranoid, don't panic. The key is to remain as innocent as a *dove*. In other words, guard your heart. Don't go out looking for evil. Stay close to Jesus, and don't let anyone—even your friends—manipulate you into sinning.

Be kind, be loving, but be smart!

## HOW DO YOU PUT THESE THREE VERY DIFFERENT PIECES OF ADVICE TOGETHER?

**READ UP: ACTS 20:28–31 • 1 CORINTHIANS 16:13–14**

# PUT WORDS IN YOUR MOUTH

**READ AHEAD: MATTHEW 10:18-20**
*Don't worry about how or what you should speak. For you will be given what to say at that hour.* Matthew 10:18

Christians love to grab onto this verse from Matthew, assuming that any time we're at a loss for words, God will intervene. No more studying, no more preparation, no more planning ahead. The words will just come automatically, courtesy of the Holy Spirit. This eliminates the need for Bible study, because God will always zap the appropriate verse into our minds at the right time. How nice of God to cover for our laziness!

Truth is, though, this is not a blanket promise. Jesus was addressing a specific situation here. He was talking to friends who would soon be hauled before kings and other authorities. They would be beaten, interrogated, and expected to explain their faith under threat of death.

None of them had known Jesus for more than a few years. And unlike Paul, who was well schooled in the Scriptures, these men were all blue-collar workers. They had no tracts or pocket New Testaments to pull out when they were in a bind. But because they were being obedient to God, being bold enough to witness for Christ, Jesus assured them God would intervene.

What does this mean for us? Obviously, there's not an open-ended guarantee that God will always bail us out when we haven't prepared ourselves. If we are living as God wants us to live, however, he will not only give us the words we need when our faith is challenged, he'll also give us the courage to say them.

## WHY DOES GOD'S DELIVERANCE NOT ALWAYS KICK IN UNTIL WE'VE PUT OUR FAITH ON THE LINE?

**READ UP: EXODUS 4:10-12 • 2 TIMOTHY 4:16-18**

# PRICE TO PAY

**READ AHEAD: MATTHEW 10:21–25**

*You will be hated by everyone because of My name. But the one who endures to the end will be delivered.* Matthew 10:22

Following Christ is not for the faint-hearted! Some may tell you that becoming a Christian guarantees you'll enjoy a problem-free existence, but Jesus shattered this illusion. In fact, he presented Christianity as not only difficult but downright dangerous!

To follow Christ in Bible times was perilous. Constant persecution separated the serious disciples from the would-be Christians. The threat of arrest, torture, and even death didn't make Christianity all that inviting. People were forced to take their commitment to Christ very seriously, because their very lives (as well as those of their family members) were on the line. Yet thousands of people considered it worth the hazards. They knew that Jesus himself was hated and persecuted, so they didn't expect to avoid persecution themselves.

Times have changed, of course, but the willingness to endure persecution still separates true disciples from the wannabes. In some parts of the world, being a Christian is still a life-threatening venture. But even though it's not physically dangerous for most of us, there's still a cost involved in following Christ. And each of us has to decide for ourselves if knowing Christ is worth the price.

Is your faith costing you anything? Are you willing to stand up for Christ even when it's unpopular? Will you remain faithful to Jesus even if it causes you to lose friends? If you're truly Christ's disciple, you will pay a price. But stand firm! The reward is worth the cost.

## WHAT DOES FOLLOWING CHRIST COST YOU TODAY?

**READ UP: PHILIPPIANS 1:29–30 • 1 PETER 4:12–19**

# LITTLE OLD ME?

### READ AHEAD: MATTHEW 10:26–31

*Aren't two sparrows sold for a penny? Yet not one of them falls to the ground without your Father's consent.* Matthew 10:29

Have you ever been in a stadium with thousands of screaming fans? Did you wonder how God could possibly know every person there? It's pretty mind-boggling! But even though there are billions of people in the world, the Bible says God knows everything there is to know about every one of us! Jesus, in fact, made a point of showing his disciples just how intimately the Father knew them.

Sparrows, for example, are among the least important creatures on earth. Their life span is extremely short. Who even notices when they die? *God does.* So why shouldn't he be more than capable of loving each and every person he's created?

What's more, he even knows the number of hairs on our heads! The truth is, God knows us better than we know ourselves. He doesn't see us as a massive crowd but as individuals, and he loves each one of us.

Jesus' disciples were going out into a hostile world. They would be mocked and threatened by hateful, dangerous people, and would even come face-to-face with demons! Jesus wanted to assure them that their heavenly Father was in control, that he loved each one of them and was watching over them.

This same promise is for you, too. Don't ever assume you're just one of the crowd. God is intimately acquainted with you and involved in your life. He knows everything about you and loves you more than you know.

## WHO'S SOMEONE YOU KNOW WHO NEEDS TO BE REMINDED OF THIS TRUTH TODAY?

### READ UP: PSALM 17:6–9 • ISAIAH 43:5–7

# TROUBLE AT HOME

**READ AHEAD: MATTHEW 10:32–36**

*Don't assume that I came to bring peace on the earth. I did not come to bring peace, but a sword.* Matthew 10:34

It's one thing when strangers—or even friends—challenge our faith. But when our own *family* opposes us, that cuts deep. Would Jesus really ask us to oppose our parents' wishes? Haven't we been commanded to honor our fathers and mothers?

Sometimes the biggest obstacle between us and obedience is the resistance we face inside our own homes. It's an obstacle some of us aren't willing to challenge because it's too painful to deal with. It's true, of course, that Jesus doesn't ask us to stop loving our families or to treat them with disrespect. But he does insist that our first loyalty be to God.

Non-Christian family members probably won't understand your choice to follow Christ. They may consider you a fanatic. They may even see your loyalty to Christ as a rejection of them. It's critical to continue loving your family, but Jesus said that if you are to be worthy of him, you must make the hard choice: God first, family second.

When your family asks you to put them before God, they are (in a sense) playing the part of your enemy. Even *Christian* family members can come between you and God. For example, if you're called into missions, your family may dissuade you because they want you nearby or because they fear the dangers you'll face. If your family is asking you to disobey God, ask him for the strength to put him first.

## WHAT HAPPENED TO THE PART ABOUT BEING PEACEMAKERS?

**READ UP: 2 CHRONICLES 15:16–18 • MICAH 7:5–7**

# BY WAY OF THE CROSS

## READ AHEAD: MATTHEW 10:37-39

*Whoever doesn't take up his cross and follow Me is not worthy of Me.* Matthew 10:38

Christians often wear crosses as jewelry around their necks or as some kind of bumper sticker on their cars, signifying their loyalty to Christ. It's probably a welcome sight for you when you see one, because it stands for your resurrected Lord. It's a victory symbol.

When Jesus referred to a cross, however, his disciples likely had a very different mental picture. No one had to tell them what a cross meant, because they'd seen plenty of them. In their day the cross was a torture device. To a condemned person, the cross was the ultimate humiliation. It meant his life was no longer his own. Any future plans he may have had were now irrelevant, because the cross he carried to his own execution would soon end his life.

Today the cross is both: it's a victory symbol *and* a sign of what Christ requires of us. When Jesus said for us to "take up" our cross, he meant that we are to turn our lives completely over to him. Our own plans are no longer important. Only what *he's* planned for us matters anymore. If we're unwilling to go where he wants us to go and to do what he asks us to do, Jesus said we're not worthy to be his followers.

If you have your future all figured out, you need to check with Jesus. Ask him what *his* plans are and begin following him today. Trust that his way is the best way . . . the way of the cross.

## WHY MUST CHRISTIANITY COME WITH A CROSS?

**READ UP: GALATIANS 6:12-14 • PHILIPPIANS 3:17-21**

# STAND-IN

**READ AHEAD: MATTHEW 10:40–42**

*The one who welcomes you welcomes Me, and the one who welcomes Me welcomes Him who sent Me.* Matthew 10:40

Why does it matter how Christians behave? Do our actions or inactions really matter as long as we're telling people the truth about Jesus? Do we, in fact, set up a false, unrealistic expectation of life by trying to be perfect all the time?

There's a good reason for Christians to act with integrity. It's because of who we represent.

There are people who may never know what Christ is like unless they see him in you. If you're a Christian, you take Christ with you everywhere you go. When you're at school or at work, Christ is with you. When you're out with your friends or talking to a stranger, Christ is with you. Whenever people meet you, they also meet Christ.

How tragic for a non-Christian to see Christ in you and be unimpressed! If you don't represent him to others in a way that honors his name, some people might never know what he's really like.

Others will be attracted to Christ when your own life shows his love, forgiveness, patience, and kindness. That's why it's so important that you always represent Christ as he is—not just with your words but also with your actions and attitudes. There are many people around you who need to receive Jesus, and you're the one who can introduce them to him. Have people been impressed with the Christ they've seen in you?

## WHAT'S THE WORST PART ABOUT PUTTING UP A CHRISTIAN ACT?

**READ UP: JOHN 12:48–50 • 2 CORINTHIANS 6:1–2**

# ONE WAY OR THE OTHER

**READ AHEAD: MATTHEW 12:25–32**

*Anyone who is not with Me is against Me, and anyone who does not gather with Me scatters.* Matthew 12:30

According to the world, there are three ways to characterize your belief in God. You can either be:

- A believer.
- An atheist (denying God's existence).
- Or an agnostic (undecided one way or the other).

You'll find the term *agnostic* in the dictionary, but you won't find it in the Bible. Jesus said there are only two options, not three. According to Jesus, whoever doesn't stand with him is automatically *against* him. There is no middle ground.

Some people prefer to remain neutral when it comes to Christ. They don't want to come right out and reject him, but they're not quite willing to accept him either. They pick and choose what they'll believe about him. They may choose to live a good life—at least by worldly standards—but they don't want to get "bogged down" by Christianity. These people are deceived, because Jesus said that in not choosing, they've made their choice. If you're not for Christ, you're against him.

If you've considered yourself in the neutral zone when it comes to trusting God, you've actually been Christ's enemy. God has given you all the information you need to make your choice for him. Choose now—before it's too late—to live for Christ.

**WHY IS THE FUZZY, GRAY AREA IN THE MIDDLE USUALLY THE MOST COWARDLY PLACE TO BE?**

**READ UP: DEUTERONOMY 30:19–20 • JOSHUA 24:14–15**

# WORDS WILL TELL

**READ AHEAD: MATTHEW 12:33–35**

*The mouth speaks from the overflow of the heart.*
Matthew 12:34

Why was Jesus so critical of the Pharisees? They tried to live by God's law. They weren't thieves or murderers. Yet Jesus had more patience for outright criminals than he had for the Pharisees. He treated tax collectors and prostitutes kindly, but he called the Pharisees a bunch of venomous snakes!

The Pharisees loved to impress people with their lengthy public prayers and their religious practices, but Jesus knew their hearts. They were preoccupied with how pious they appeared on the outside, while on the inside they were critical, judgmental, and proud. Their goal as religious teachers was not to lead others closer to God but to show everyone how spiritual they were. They pitied everyone else for being wretched sinners, but they were blind to their own sin.

Self-deception is a crafty enemy. We may think we're fooling everyone around us with the spiritual act we put on, but we're the ones who are usually deceived . . . because it's hard to keep what's in our hearts from coming out through our words. If we're filled with jealousy, we can't help cutting down others. If we're judgmental, we criticize people more often than not. In unguarded moments our anger slips out in bitter, hurtful words.

There's no sense wasting our energy trying to say all the right things if our hearts aren't right with Jesus. When we're square with him, good things will follow naturally.

## WHAT ARE YOUR OPTIONS FOR DEALING WITH YOUR OWN HYPOCRISY?

**READ UP: LUKE 18:9–14 • JAMES 3:7–12**

# WHAT'D YOU SAY?

### READ AHEAD: MATTHEW 12:36-37

*I tell you that on the day of judgment people will have to account for every careless word they speak.* Matthew 12:36

Speaking without thinking is like playing with a loaded gun, and careless words are its bullets. When the gun goes off and injures someone, the damage is done. You can retrieve the bullet, but you can't undo the harm it caused.

Have you ever hurt someone's feelings with careless words, then shrugged it off because your target was just being overly sensitive? Have you ever spread gossip about someone, embellishing it a little to spice up the story? Have you cut down a friend's self-confidence with your "all in fun" jabs? Have you dishonored God by using his name disrespectfully even though you knew better?

Most of us will admit that we don't always choose our words wisely. But if we really understood the power of our words, we'd never shoot them off as carelessly as we do. God knows how damaging our words can be, and he takes them far more seriously than we do.

Jesus cautioned us, in fact, that one day we'll all be required to account for "every careless word" we've spoken. Imagine standing before holy God in heaven as every stray word we ever spoke on earth is revealed!

If you tend to shoot off your mouth, ask God today to help you gain control over your tongue. Begin choosing your words wisely—thinking before you speak—so that you will have no need for regrets.

## HOW SURPRISING TO YOU IS THIS LITTLE WARNING FROM JESUS?

### READ UP: LEVITICUS 5:4-5 • 2 CHRONICLES 19:4-10

# NOW I GET IT

**READ AHEAD: MATTHEW 13:3-9**

*He told them many things in parables, saying: "Consider the sower who went out to sow . . ."* Matthew 13:3

Good teachers don't just deliver lectures. They help their students picture the material. They speak in terms their listeners will understand.

When Jesus had an important lesson for his disciples or for the crowds who gathered around him, he showed them what he wanted them to know by painting word pictures for them. He talked about things that were part of their experience, such as farming and fishing, food and nature.

One parable he used, which was designed to teach his followers about genuine faith, talked about four types of soil, all of which received the same seed. He compared this to the four ways people respond to the same gospel:

- Satan prevents some from understanding the gospel.
- Others respond immediately, but soon fall away.
- Others accept Christ but fall victim to worldly pressures.
- But some hear it, receive it, and grow in their faith.

The first three types of soil produce no crop, but the fourth type of soil represents those who make a difference in God's kingdom.

Consider each of the four soil types Jesus talked about in this parable. Then think about your own response to the gospel. Has God's Word produced everything it's supposed to in your life?

## WHAT KINDS OF PARALLELS COULD YOU USE TO TELL PEOPLE ABOUT GOD?

**READ UP: MARK 4:33–34 • JOHN 16:25–33**

# FAITH IN FAITH?

## READ AHEAD: MATTHEW 17:14–21

*If you have faith the size of a mustard seed, you will tell this mountain, "Move from here to there."* Matthew 17:20

Faith is measured by quality, not quantity. It's not how *much* faith we have that counts, but where we put it.

Sometimes we put our faith in our *faith*, instead of in God. We think if we just *believe* hard enough, we'll get whatever we want. We trust in ourselves rather than in God. But faith by itself is as worthless as a solar-powered flashlight or an inflatable dartboard. The power to move mountains is in God, not in our faith.

When the disciples asked Jesus why they hadn't been able to cast out demons with complete success, he told them they had been exercising false confidence in their own faith. They had grown to believe in themselves and their ability to do things for God, instead of believing in his ability to work through them. They were treating their faith like a magic wand they could pull out whenever they needed another miracle. They had placed their faith in *faith* rather than in God.

Be careful you don't fall under this same misconception. Don't even *try* to work up enough faith, thinking that at some point God will say, "Now that you've reached the minimum faith requirement, you're ready to move mountains." Instead, put your faith where it belongs—not in yourself, but in God. Then stand aside and watch him move the mountain for you!

**WHAT ARE THE BIGGEST HAZARDS OF PUTTING OUR FAITH IN OUR OWN FAITH?**

## READ UP: ACTS 8:18–23 • ROMANS 4:18–21

# SUCCESS STRATEGIES

**READ AHEAD: MATTHEW 20:23–28**

*The Son of Man did not come to be served, but to serve, and to give His life—a ransom for many.* Matthew 20:28

*Wanted:* Male or female to be a model of success for the world.

*Qualifications:* Must be attractive, charming, bright, and physically fit. Only the wealthy need apply. Money can be either earned or inherited but not stolen. You may be required to show evidence of greatness, such as how many persons are serving you. Good dose of luck helpful but not essential. Fame definitely an asset. Send resumé, full-length picture, medical records, and list of important friends.

*Wanted:* Male or female to be a model of success for Christians.

*Qualifications:* Must be kind, patient, and generous. Good dose of humility essential. Selfish applicants need not apply. May be required to show evidence of greatness, such as how many people you're serving and how you've been persecuted for your Christian life. Only servants will be considered. Send resumé—no picture or medical records or list of influential friends necessary. It doesn't matter what you look like or how healthy you are or who you know.

See the difference?

If anyone had a right to be served, it was Jesus. Yet he didn't come to be served; he came to serve. So if you're looking for a genuine model of success, you'll find it in Jesus. If you want to have the success he had, you'll have to live like he did—as a servant.

## WHO OR WHAT DO YOU SOMETIMES SERVE BESIDES JESUS?

**READ UP: ISAIAH 42:1–3 • 2 CORINTHIANS 8:8–9**

# FIRST THING

### READ AHEAD: MATTHEW 22:34–38

*This is the greatest and most important commandment.*
Matthew 22:38

The Pharisee in this passage had a question for Jesus: "Which commandment in the law is the greatest?" It was a loaded question, designed to trap Jesus and discredit him.

No doubt, the Pharisee expected Jesus would choose one of the Ten Commandments over the other nine, opening the door for debate. Then the religious expert figured he'd have this unschooled carpenter's son right where he wanted him—no match for his expertise. This was going to be one easy victory!

But Jesus showed who the expert really was. He condensed all Ten Commandments into one statement that targeted the Pharisees' most vulnerable spot—the heart of their obedience.

The Pharisees were adept at keeping the letter of the law, but fell pitifully short in following the spirit of it. They did all the right things for all the wrong reasons. And in God's eyes, all this self-serving law-abiding amounted to sin. God expected them to obey his commands because they *loved* him, not because they were trying to be perfect. He was more concerned with their hearts than with their actions.

Sometimes we're like the Pharisees. We make Christianity much too complicated. But God asks only one thing of us—love. If we devote our hearts, minds, and souls to him, we will fulfill the law as he meant it to be followed, and everything else will fall into place.

## WHY DOES THIS ONE COMMANDMENT PRETTY MUCH SUM UP ALL THE OTHERS?

### READ UP: DEUTERONOMY 10:12–20 • 1 CORINTHIANS 2:6–9

# NEW NEIGHBORHOOD

**READ AHEAD: MATTHEW 22:37–40**

*The second is like it: "Love your neighbor as yourself."*
Matthew 22:39

When you consider Jesus' audience, his message was revolutionary! The Old Testament law was *everything* to the Pharisees. They devoted their entire lives to following it to the letter. But now Jesus was telling them that all their efforts were futile unless they loved their neighbors.

The Pharisees weren't in the habit of loving their neighbors. They were actually in the habit of criticizing, judging, and pitying them. After all, their neighborhood included some pretty unsavory characters—prostitutes, beggars, and tax collectors. These were nasty, sinful people. I mean, the Pharisees had their standards.

But God has standards, too—high standards. He expects us to treat others exactly as we want to be treated ourselves. It's tempting to avoid those we find hard to love, choosing instead to stick with people who are more like us. That way we can still be loving, but it doesn't really put us out too much.

God, however, expects us to show love to our neighbors no matter who they are. Jesus used the word *love* as a verb—an action word. We often think of it as a noun—something we have, not something we do.

Do you find some people impossible to love? Don't waste your time trying to decide whether someone is worthy of your time and attention. Instead, ask God to help you act lovingly toward everyone you encounter, even when it's difficult.

## WHAT DOES LOVING YOUR UNLOVELY NEIGHBORS LOOK LIKE?

**READ UP: 1 PETER 1:22–25 • 1 JOHN 4:7–8**

# HUMBLY SPEAKING

**READ AHEAD: MATTHEW 23:8–12**

*The greatest among you will be your servant.*
Matthew 23:11

We can always count on the Bible to turn human reasoning inside out. Such thinking is nonsense to the world, but it's crucial for Christians to understand truths like the ones in today's feature verse if we're to live as Christ desires. Today, let's tackle this concept of humility, seeing it the way Jesus sees it.

Nobody is born humble. Humility is a trait we all have to learn. We humans instinctively want to present our best possible picture to the world, so we go to great lengths to hide our weaknesses and highlight our strengths.

Sometimes we go even further by trying to make a good impression at someone else's expense. We're threatened when others receive praise, so we set out to prove that we, not they, deserve the attention.

This is the way we've always done things. Life has taught us that if we don't promote ourselves, no one else will. But God says the opposite is true: if we act proud and build ourselves up, we'll be brought down. Yet if we stop worrying about impressing everyone, seeking to be genuinely humble instead, others will end up thinking highly of us.

If you've been preoccupied with your image, if you've been trying to impress those around you, you've been duped by the world's thinking. From now on, humble yourself and put others first. That's God's way. And when you think about it, it really does make more sense than the way the world does things.

**WHAT'S THE FIRST STEP YOU COULD TAKE TO BEGIN HONING YOUR HUMILITY TODAY?**

**READ UP: 1 SAMUEL 2:3–9 • LUKE 1:51–53**

# WHAT STRUCK YOU THE MOST ABOUT JESUS' INSTRUCTIONS?

# DEEP-DOWN DEVOTION

Daniel was born into nobility. Therefore, he should have possessed all the advantages, pleasures, and opportunities that came with life in the upper class. When Daniel was a teenager in Jerusalem, however, his nation was invaded by Babylon (the world superpower of that day), whose ruler, Nebuchadnezzar, stripped Israel of most of its wealth.

In 605 B.C. this conquering king arrested Israel's finest young people and had them brought to Babylon. His goal was to brainwash them into forgetting their heritage and their belief in God, forcing them to adopt the pagan religion of the Babylonians.

One of these young men was a guy you know.

His Hebrew name, Daniel, meant "God is my judge," But he was given the Babylonian name Belteshazzar, meaning "protect his life." He was offered every luxury the king could provide in an attempt to coerce him into giving up his religion.

But Daniel refused, committing himself to remain true to God, even if he was the only one to do so. As a result, he ended up in some pretty frightening situations.

Yet God honored Daniel's commitment, granting him unusual wisdom and giving him a prominent place in world affairs. When conniving men grew jealous and sought to destroy him, God saved him from certain death. Steadfastly throughout his life, Daniel refused to compromise his faith in God—even for the most powerful people in the world—and God blessed him greatly in return.

Daniel stands out as a young person who remained true to God in the face of great danger. We'll spend the next five days getting to know better this faithful servant of God.

# ALL-NEW SURROUNDINGS

## READ AHEAD: DANIEL 1:1-7

*Nebuchadnezzar carried them to the land of Babylon, to the house of his god.* Daniel 1:2

If you were to move to a new country—one with a strange language, different customs, and foreign foods—how do you think you'd adjust?

Daniel had no choice about moving. Nebuchadnezzar, the powerful Babylonian king, had conquered Jerusalem. He had forcibly taken young people from the wealthiest families and brought them to the distant city of Babylon. Daniel had been taken from his family, his home, and his country to live in a hostile land filled with idol worshipers.

Everything was different now—the language, the religion, the laws. Everything except one thing—God. And Daniel found that God was just as real to him in Babylon as he had been in Jerusalem. Daniel's enemies could remove his parents and his friends, but they could not take God away from him.

God's presence made all the difference to Daniel. That's why he was able to approach his new life with confidence rather than fear.

If you're experiencing troublesome changes right now, remember that one thing hasn't changed: God is still with you. You may feel all alone, but God loves you, and he's ready to help you, no matter what you're facing next. You may not always have your parents or friends nearby to help you, but God has promised that he will always be there with you, wherever you are.

## WHAT KINDS OF NEW SITUATIONS ARE COMING UP IN YOUR LIFE?

**READ UP: JOSHUA 1:7-9 • ISAIAH 41:8-10**

# NOT ME

### READ AHEAD: DANIEL 1:8–16

*Daniel determined that he would not defile himself with the king's food or with the wine he drank.* Daniel 1:8

If Daniel had just been examining the facts, they would have looked something like this:

• Fact: He was far from home, facing the temptation to do things he knew were wrong.

• Fact: His parents would never find out if he gave in to temptation.

• Fact: Most of his friends were sinning and encouraging him to join them anyway.

• Fact: The most powerful king on earth wanted him to give up his beliefs in return for wealth and power. That would be a welcome change from his current status as a foreigner in a hostile land.

The facts seemed to indicate that it was in Daniel's best interest to abandon his faith and take up this foreign religion. But Daniel had made a commitment in his heart not to compromise his faith in God, no matter how tempting it was, no matter what price he would have to pay for his obedience.

It's something to think about, isn't it? "Everybody seems to be doing whatever they please . . . Mom and Dad will never find out . . . There are certain rewards for following the crowd."

"*But* . . . I've made a commitment not to compromise my Christianity no matter what others do." God will bless you for faithfulness like that.

## WHEN DO YOU FIND THIS KIND OF AGAINST-THE-FLOW COURAGE THE HARDEST TO MUSTER UP?

### READ UP: PSALM 112:5–8 • ISAIAH 12:2–6

# EVEN IF

**READ AHEAD: DANIEL 3:14-18**

*But even if He does not rescue us . . . we will not serve your gods or worship the gold statue you set up.* Daniel 3:18

Would you continue to trust God if you asked him for something and his answer was no? Is your faith only strong when things are going your way, or do you continue to trust him when things seem to be falling apart?

Daniel had three friends who had promised not to make deals with God. They each had made a commitment that regardless of what everyone else did, they would remain faithful to him.

They soon had an opportunity to prove it. The king issued an order that every person in the nation must bow down to a golden idol. And so the instant the king's musicians began to play, the massive crowd dropped collectively to the ground in deference to the king's god. But to Nebuchadnezzar's displeasure, Daniel's three friends remained standing.

The king summoned the infidels and gave them one last chance to comply with his order. Still, they stood firm. Nebuchadnezzar was furious! For their treason they were to be thrown into a gigantic furnace, which had been stoked to seven times its normal temperature. He was determined to get rid of these stubborn foreigners!

Then came perhaps the greatest statement of faith found in the Bible: *Even if God doesn't miraculously save us, we will still trust him.* That's real faith—not based upon getting what we want but on knowing who God is and trusting in his love and his will.

## WHAT DOES THIS COURAGEOUS VERSE MAKE YOU WANT TO DO?

**READ UP: JOB 13:13-15 • PSALM 27:1-3**

# CAN'T MAKE IT STICK

**READ AHEAD: DANIEL 6:1-5**

*They could find no charge or corruption, for he was trustworthy, and no negligence or corruption was found in him.* Daniel 6:4

What would happen if your enemies set out to find every damaging piece of information they could find about you? What if they followed you to see where you spent your time? What if they tapped your phone and eavesdropped on your conversations? What if they checked your bank account to see where you spend your money? What if they interviewed your classmates or coworkers, looking for someone with some dirt on you? Would they come up with some embarrassing information?

That's what Daniel's enemies tried to do. They desperately wanted to dig up some incriminating evidence on him to make him lose his job. But Daniel had nothing to fear. The worst thing they could come up with was that he prayed a lot!

There's incredible freedom in living a clean life. It eliminates the need to keep secrets or to worry about what might be exposed. It removes the vice grip that guilt can hold on your conscience.

Perhaps you've already done things that, if revealed, would cause you shame. But although you can't change the past, you can still start fresh. Ask God to forgive your past sins and help you begin a life of integrity. Each time you face a questionable decision, ask yourself: "Would I be ashamed if what I'm about to do were made public?" Then you'll be able to enjoy the tremendous freedom that comes from a pure lifestyle.

## HOW CAN YOU LET GO OF THE GUILT FROM PAST SINS—AND BREAK THE CYCLE OF BAD HABITS?

**READ UP: ROMANS 3:23-26 • 1 PETER 4:1-6**

# A PATTERN OF PRAYER

## READ AHEAD: DANIEL 9:20–23

*At the beginning of your petitions an answer went out.*
Daniel 9:23

This was not the first time God had heard Daniel pray, because Daniel apparently prayed all the time. He prayed when things were going well. He prayed when he was having problems. He prayed just because he enjoyed talking with God.

Daniel's faithfulness and his love for God must have earned him high regard in heaven, because no sooner were the words of his prayer in chapter 9 out of his mouth than God quickly sent an angel to minister to him.

Sometimes we neglect to pray for long periods of time. When everything is going our way, we forget to thank God. We get busy and don't really see the need to spend time talking with him. Then a problem pops up and we need help—now! We pray fervently and want God's answer immediately. We feel frustrated if our prayer isn't answered promptly!

We need to follow Daniel's example. God responded to Daniel's need even before Daniel finished his prayer. Their relationship was that close. The best part for Daniel wasn't even the speediness of God's answer but the security he had in knowing he was highly respected by God.

Do you pray because you enjoy talking with God, or do you just pray when you need something? Strive to be like Daniel, and enjoy spending time with God in prayer no matter what your situation.

## HOW WOULD YOU CHARACTERIZE YOUR RELATIONSHIP WITH GOD RIGHT NOW?

## READ UP: MATTHEW 7:7–11 • 2 THESSALONIANS 1:11–12

# WHAT'S STANDING BETWEEN YOU AND DANIEL'S COURAGE?

# WANT TO START AGAIN?

It's more than just the music, the parties, and the fireworks that make a day like New Year's Eve fun and exciting. It's also the realization that starting the next morning, a whole new year stretches out before you, unstained, untouched, twelve new months to improve on the ones you're leaving behind.

So bring that kind of feeling to this last, six-day section of devotionals. If you've chugged your way through this book—stopping and starting, getting behind, succeeding in spurts but failing in others—approach these final readings as your chance to start afresh. Promise yourself that with God's help and power, you're going to stick with this Christian life no matter how difficult it can be at times. You're going to open yourself wider than ever, ready to receive and experience the rewards of walking with Jesus.

Life is not a forty-yard dash but a long-distance marathon. It's not won in flashes of brilliance but over many days of steady progress. It's a long haul filled with good and bad, with victories and losses, but never without hope that today and tomorrow can be days of renewal.

These final few devotionals are a handful of big biblical ideas to remember when you're ready to rebuild and refresh. Are you needing a new start today . . . even this close to the end of this devotional book? Receive God's ever-present offer of grace, and begin again with his forgiveness and power to carry you.

That's what we mean when we call Christian living an *experience!*

# DAY AFTER DAY

## READ AHEAD: LUKE 2:36–38

*She did not leave the temple complex, serving God night and day with fastings and prayers.* Luke 2:37

You've probably heard about Anna. She's the elderly woman we often read about at Christmastime, the one who prayed her entire life for the Messiah to come. Day after day, year after year, decade after decade, she prayed without giving up. And finally, when she was very old, she saw the Christ child with her own eyes—the answer to her prayers. Anna serves as an example of faithfulness over the long haul!

We're often quick to assume God has decided not to answer our prayers. We might pray for an unbelieving friend for a few months or maybe even for a year. But time passes, and our friend doesn't become a Christian, so we lose interest and abandon our prayer. We assume our friend will never come to know Christ or it would have already happened by now. How easily discouraged we get when we don't see results soon enough to suit us!

Our problem is, we pray according to our own agenda, not God's. It's vital to remember that God works by his own timetable, not ours.

Have you been praying for someone who doesn't know Christ? Have you been praying for one of God's promises to come about in your life? Don't set a time limit on how soon God should answer. Keep praying and don't get discouraged. In the long run, when God answers your prayer, you'll enjoy a double blessing—because you'll have learned faithfulness in the long-term as well.

## WHAT DOES GOD DO IN THE LONG HAUL THAT WE'D NEVER EXPERIENCE IN THE SHORT RUN?

**READ UP: LUKE 21:12–19 • ROMANS 5:3–5**

# NOTHING'S IMPOSSIBLE

**READ AHEAD: JEREMIAH 32:17-19**

*You Yourself made the heavens and earth by Your great power. . . . Nothing is too difficult for You!* Jeremiah 32:17

Exactly how powerful is the God we serve? We *talk* about his power. We *hear* about his power. We even *sing* about his power. But do we really *experience* his power?

Jeremiah needed a miracle. He was in prison for confronting the king of Judah with a word from God, just as God had told him to do. Everyone was angry with this truth-telling prophet. From the heads of state down to the peasants, everyone in Judah hated him and mocked him for saying unpopular things.

But as Jeremiah was praying—instead of dwelling in self-pity on his situation—he looked at the sky and contemplated how powerful God must be to create the heavens and the earth. Then he reviewed in his mind all the miracles God had done through the ages.

Jeremiah had heard, of course, about the many mighty acts of God performed throughout history, but now he needed to see one for himself. He needed to experience God's power. God was faithful to Jeremiah. Not only did he free Jeremiah from captivity, but everything God had predicted occurred exactly as he said it would.

Don't settle for mere talk about God's power, or for books and songs about his power. Ask him to show you for yourself. If God has given you a task that looks impossible, do it anyway. Then you can experience his power accomplishing his will through your life.

> WHAT PARTS OF YOUR CURRENT DIFFICULTIES ARE IRRELEVANT WHEN SEEN AGAINST GOD'S POWER?

**READ UP: 2 KINGS 3:16-20 • MATTHEW 19:25-30**

# QUICK ON THE TRIGGER

**READ AHEAD: LUKE 9:51-56**

*Lord, do you want us to call down fire from heaven to consume them?* Luke 9:54

There had been bitter animosity between the Jewish people and the Samaritans for years, so it probably didn't surprise the disciples that they weren't well received in Samaria.

However, they weren't about to stand by and see Jesus mistreated and not welcomed in this Samaritan village.

So James and John quickly came up with a plan to repay these rude half-breeds for their lack of hospitality: "Let's teach them a lesson! Let's pull off a huge miracle and destroy the village in the process. Then they'll be sorry!" Talk about overreacting!

Jesus, of course, had other plans. He rebuked his zealous friends, and they carried on with their journey.

Fast-forward, though, to Acts 8:14, where the Bible tells us that the Samaritans later accepted the gospel. And guess who was sent by God to pray with them? Peter and John! As they prayed with these Gentile believers, John, the recovering pyromaniac, must have felt more than a little twinge of guilt. If he'd had his way, his current prayer partners would have been roasted alive years before!

Only God knows what's in a person's heart. Only God understands why people say what they say and do what they do. So if you'll take your hurts to God and give others the benefit of the doubt, you'll save yourself from doing things you'll later regret. In addition, you may see God do a miracle in the end!

## HOW HAVE YOU BEEN BURNED BEFORE BY MISREADING SOMEONE'S MOTIVES?

**READ UP: PSALM 69:5-6 • ROMANS 11:17-20**

# WAIT UP

**READ AHEAD: PSALM 27:7–14**

*Wait for the Lord; be courageous and let your heart be strong. Wait for the Lord.* Psalm 27:14

Waiting is one of the hardest things to do in all the world! If you have to wait for someone who's late, or if you're expecting something important in the mail, or if you're waiting for the phone to ring, it can almost drive you crazy! Waiting means you're not in control. Someone else—besides you—is getting to determine what happens next.

Waiting on the Lord, however, is a different matter. When God delays in giving you something, he has a good reason. It's not that he doesn't love you or that he wants to make you squirm. It's a matter of timing.

Waiting on God reminds us of just how much our lives depend on him. Every day we wait is another day to realize how helpless we are apart from his strength. This is why waiting on God can be one of the most spiritually rewarding things we ever do. Waiting on God doesn't mean sitting around doing nothing. It involves action on our part:

- We should pray.
- We should continue doing what God told us last.
- We should watch for what he does next.
- We should check our hearts to see if sin is hindering God's answer.

If you're waiting on God for something right now, don't consider the time an idle, frustrating experience. Trust that he loves you . . . and that his answer will come.

## WHAT PROOF DO YOU HAVE THAT GOD IS WORKING HIS PERFECT WILL IN YOUR LIFE?

**READ UP: PROVERBS 8:34–35 • ROMANS 8:26–29**

# FUTURE-TENSE REALITY

**READ AHEAD: PHILIPPIANS 1:3-6**

*He who started a good work in you will carry it on to completion until the day of Christ Jesus.* Philippians 1:6

In the book of Revelation, John described Christ as the Alpha and the Omega, meaning "the beginning" and "the end" (Revelation 22:13). In other words, God is eternal. He is not bound by time. He doesn't just *see* the future; he's *in* the future, just as he's in the past and present. When God begins something in your life, he already knows how it will end, because he is there already.

When you became a Christian, God's Holy Spirit began the work of making you like Christ. He continues to work in your life even now to bring about holiness, and he will continue to do so until you arrive in heaven to spend eternity face-to-face with him. You can be absolutely confident that whatever Christ begins in you, he will finish.

If you've received a word from God about something he wants to do in your life, trust that he will make it happen. Don't let circumstances discourage you. God isn't intimidated by circumstances. Obey him with confidence, because God always completes what he starts.

God has seen your future. He knows what will happen. If you have sensed God saying something to you—something that's in line with what his Word already says—know that God is perfectly capable of doing his part. Immediately adjust your life to what he has told you, and then watch to see how God makes everything he said become a reality.

## WHAT DIFFERENCE WOULD THIS ATTITUDE MAKE IN YOUR LIFE?

**READ UP: PSALM 138:7-8 • 1 CORINTHIANS 1:4-9**

# LET'S DO IT

## READ AHEAD: ISAIAH 5:1–7

*What more could I have done for My vineyard than I did?*
Isaiah 5:4

Sometimes we feel completely inadequate to do what God expects us to do. We know he wants us to grow as Christians and to show signs of maturity, yet we feel helpless to change the way we think or the way we behave.

The truth is, God doesn't ask us to do anything on our own. He always provides the right tools.

Isaiah told of a vine grower and his quest for a lush harvest of grapes. This farmer spared no effort or expense in planting his vineyard. He found the most fertile land, cleared it of all stones and obstructions, then planted only the choicest vines in it. He built a watchtower so he could see intruders coming and protect his crop. He even built a wine vat and waited in readiness for the bumper crop he knew would come.

When harvest time came, however, he discovered only worthless grapes. Despite his best efforts, these grapes had no value.

God has given us so much. He has given us the church for support, encouragement, and fellowship. He has given us free access to his written Word. Above all, he has given us himself. As Christians, we have the Holy Spirit living within us, guiding us and giving us strength. In return, God wants us to produce good fruit. He wants us to be holy. He wants us to trust him.

God has done his part. Now he waits in anticipation to see what fruit we will produce.

## HOW WOULD YOUR LIFE BE DIFFERENT IF GOD HAD YOUR WHOLE HEART?

**READ UP: COLOSSIANS 2:6–15 • REVELATION 22:14–17**

# ANYTHING ELSE YOU FEEL LIKE SAYING?

www.BroadmanHolman.com

## Don't miss these other great resources for students.

| | | | |
|---|---|---|---|
| Am I The One? | 0-8054-2573-X | Vision Moments | 0-8054-2725-2 |
| Beyond the Game | 0-8054-3042-3 | They All Can't Be Right | 0-8054-3031-8 |
| Call Waiting | 0-8054-3125-X | TQ120a | 0-8054-3068-7 |
| Plan de Acción (Survival Guide Spanish) | 0-8054-3045-8 | TQ120b | 0-8054-3069-5 |
| Getting Deep: Understand What You | | TQ120c | 0-8054-3070-9 |
| Believe about God and Why | 0-8054-2554-3 | TruthQuest™ Devotional Journal | 0-8054-3800-9 |
| Getting Deep in the Book of James | 0-8054-2853-4 | TruthQuest™ Prayer Journal | 0-8054-3777-0 |
| Getting Deep in the Book of Luke | 0-8054-2852-6 | TruthQuest™ Share Jesus Without | |
| Getting Deep in the Book of Revelation | 0-8054-2854-2 | Fear New Testament (HCSB®) | 1-58640-013-4 |
| Getting Deep in the Book of Romans | 0-8054-2857-7 | | |
| He'll Forgive Me Anyway | 0-8054-2752-X | **TruthQuest™ Inductive Student Bibles (NLT)** | |
| Impact | 0-8054-2584-5 | Paperback Bible | 1-55819-848-2 |
| Jesusology | 0-8054-3049-0 | Hardcover Bible | 1-55819-855-5 |
| Living Loud | 0-8054-2482-2 | Black Leather with Slide Tab | 1-55819-843-1 |
| Something From Nothing | 0-8054-2779-1 | Blue Leather with Slide Tab | 1-55819-849-0 |
| Strikezone | 0-8054-3087-3 | Paperback with Expedition Bible Case | 1-55819-928-4 |
| Survival Guide | 0-8054-2485-7 | Expedition Bible Case Only | 1-55819-929-2 |